JORI AGUILAR SAMS

What Every Woman Should Know

Volume I – A Journey of Liberty: An Essential Study Guide for Understanding Gender Equality

First published by Writeious Books 2021

Copyright © 2021 by Jori Aguilar Sams

All rights reserved. No part of this publication may be reproduced, stored or transmitted in any form or by any means, electronic, mechanical, photocopying, recording, scanning, or otherwise without written permission from the publisher. It is illegal to copy this book, post it to a website, or distribute it by any other means without permission.

Jori Aguilar Sams asserts the moral right to be identified as the author of this work.

Jori Aguilar Sams has no responsibility for the persistence or accuracy of URLs for external or third-party Internet Websites referred to in this publication and does not guarantee that any content on such Websites is, or will remain, accurate or appropriate.

Designations used by companies to distinguish their products are often claimed as trademarks. All brand names and product names used in this book and on its cover are trade names, service marks, trademarks and registered trademarks of their respective owners. The publishers and the book are not associated with any product or vendor mentioned in this book. None of the companies referenced within the book have endorsed the book.

Third edition

ISBN: 978-0-9855367-0-1

This book was professionally typeset on Reedsy. Find out more at reedsy.com

This book is dedicated to my mother, who throughout my younger years made countless sacrifices. She showed me by example what it was to be a strong, independent woman. Through her, I learned how to face adversity.

To the Holy Spirit, who generously and without bias, imparts wisdom.

This job has been given to me to do. Therefore, it is a gift. Therefore, it is a privilege. Therefore, it is an offering I may make to God.

—Elizabeth Elliot

Contents

Introduction	iii
Chapter One	1
In the Beginning	1
Chapter Two	14
After the Fall	14
Chapter Three	35
Patriarchy	35
Chapter Four	49
Beginning to Understand the Beginning	49
Chapter Five	64
The Glory of the Law	64
Chapter Six	78
Women and the Household of God	78
Chapter Seven	98
The Household and the Bride	98
Chapter Eight	119
The Church and the Woman; the Woman and the Man	119
Chapter Nine	134
Making the Bride Beautiful	134
Chapter Ten	150
The Silence of Women	150
Chapter Eleven	164
After the Testaments	164

Chapter Twelve	176
The Trail Ahead for Women in the Church	176
Conclusion	189
Afterword	191
Bibliography for What Every Woman Should Know Volumes I and...	194
Thank You!	211
About the Author	213
Also by Jori Aguilar Sams	214

Introduction

The genesis of this journey eludes a pinpoint origin; rather, it burgeoned from seeds sown long ago, finally taking root and blossoming. I trace its nascent stirrings to a moment etched in memory, back when I was just eleven. Standing in the hallway, ensnared by illness, my greasy hair cascading down my back, and my eyes hollowed by perpetual sickness, I awaited my father's arrival after his summons. His visit yielded naught but the weekly stipend, a meager acknowledgment of maternal care that felt hollow amidst my tears as he drove away.

That poignant juncture ignited a quest for more profound truths, a yearning beyond the confines of sickness and sorrow, beyond the mundane facade of existence. For years, I found solace in fleeing the specters that haunted my parents, yet clarity eluded me until the eve of my mother's passing. In the intimate hours preceding her departure, a revelation dawned, altering the trajectory of my search, though her absence soon after left a profound void.

Since then, I've sought refuge at the feet of Christ, weary from the relentless pursuit of understanding. The scars borne from early trials left an indelible mark, fostering a heightened sensitivity to unseen forces and prompting a lifetime of inquiry. Through the anguish and toil, a journey of enlightenment unfolded, propelled by a fervent hope that amidst the pain, a greater purpose awaited.

The path to enlightenment proved arduous, marked by moments of despair and wasted energy, yet amidst the struggle, a thirst for knowledge and wisdom emerged. Unexpectedly, I discovered within myself a scholar, driven by a divine imperative to explore the parity between man and woman through the prism of God's word. This manuscript, birthed from agony and determination, bears witness to my earnest endeavor, a testament to my unwavering commitment to seek divine guidance.

As I lay bare my soul, I acknowledge the melodrama that permeates my narrative. For years, I've wielded words as my arsenal, crafting diverse works across genres in pursuit of artistic resonance. In this endeavor, I aim to traverse the vast expanse of women's equality, delving into the genesis of societal constructs and the transformative power of faith.

Through meticulous research and introspection, I endeavor to unravel the tapestry of gender equality, drawing from the depths of scripture and historical context to illuminate the evolving role of women. From the dawn of creation to the modern-day, I explore the intricacies of marriage, societal norms, and the enduring struggle for parity.

In laying bare the complexities of femininity and faith, I invite readers to embark on a journey of introspection and discovery. Though some revelations may prove unsettling, they possess the potential to reshape perceptions and ignite a fervent pursuit of truth. With each chapter, I challenge readers to confront preconceptions, to delve deeper into scripture, and to emerge enlightened and empowered.

In this pursuit of truth, I make no apologies for the intensity of my convictions, nor do I shy away from controversy. With unwavering resolve, I press forward, a pioneer driven by a divine mandate to challenge the status quo and champion the cause of equality.

As I commit these words to paper, I do so with humility, acknowledging that every revelation gained has been wrought through suffering. May this manuscript serve as a beacon of hope, a catalyst for change, and a testament to the enduring power of faith amidst adversity

Chapter One

In the Beginning

T he Creation proclaims outright the Creator; for the very heavens, as the Prophet says, declare the glory of God with their unutterable words. We see the universal harmony in the wondrous sky and on the wondrous earth; how elements essentially opposed to each other are all woven together in an ineffable union to serve one common end, each contributing its particular force to maintain the whole. —Macrina the Younger

In my forty-year odyssey through various Protestant congregations, I've often found myself feeling like a mere shadow, relegated to the sidelines of what sometimes resembles a rigid social club. Male figures predominantly occupy positions of

authority, leaving me to ponder my own visibility within these walls. Despite the rhetoric of equality, the reality seldom matched, leaving me to question the very essence of what it means to be treated as an equal. These feelings of marginalization were not occasional occurrences but rather constant companions, like shadows that refuse to dissipate in the light of day.

The directive for women to remain silent in church, attributed to the Apostle Paul, added another layer of confusion and frustration to my journey. As someone hailing from the West, where women enjoy more freedoms than in many other parts of the world, I've had the luxury of questioning the societal norms imposed upon me. Yet, even amidst these relative freedoms, true equality remains an elusive goal, hindered by societal upheavals and the erosion of familial bonds.

Progress and the Industrial Revolution

The Industrial Revolution, often hailed as a harbinger of progress, brought with it a myriad of inventions that eased the burden of household chores. While the sewing and washing machines undoubtedly lightened the load of daily drudgery, they also seemed to usher in an era of emptiness—a void that no amount of convenience could fill. Loneliness and depression became unwelcome bedfellows in the age of industrialization, hinting at a deeper loss of connection to something greater than ourselves.

In the digital age, where screens dominate our lives, women continue to benefit from innovations like the internet, which has opened doors to vast opportunities globally. However, this unprecedented access to technology has come at a cost, with social skills and the value of life itself often taking a backseat to the allure of virtual connection.

Delving into history, particularly the dynamics of family life and societal structures, has become a source of fascination and enlightenment for me. Even with the little I've gleaned, I've begun to apply these truths as anchors for healthier perspectives on my purpose and role as a woman.

My quest for understanding has revealed profound insights into the dynamics between men and women, rooted in the essence of human nature and divine design. In contemplating the origins of creation and the intentions behind God's laws, I've come to recognize their role in delineating boundaries within a fallen world, aimed at protecting the innocent and restoring harmony between humanity and the divine.

God's Ultimate Plan

Yet, amidst the strife and discord of human existence, there remains a glimmer of hope—a hope rooted in the belief that God's ultimate plan for humanity will prevail, guiding us back to a state of shalom, where we walk in communion with our Creator once more.

Daily life underwent a seismic shift. Initially, God ordained mankind to rule over all earthly creatures, save for Himself. However, after the fall, humanity's desire for dominion turned inward, leading to the inception of city dwelling and the birth of civilizations. These societies, veering from God's design, crafted their own narratives through myth, legend, and politics, perpetuating a cycle of dominance and survival.

Yet, amidst this tumult, God's sovereign plan remained unwavering. In Genesis, we witness the beginning of His strategy as He calls forth a chosen people, exemplified in the covenant with Abraham. This mission, encapsulated in Christopher Wright's Mission Triangle, aimed to extend God's blessings from Israel to all of humanity and the earth, shaping the course of history.

However, human frailty and rebellion clouded this divine mission, as Israel turned inward, misconstruing God's intentions. It was in this pivotal moment that God intervened, manifesting in the person of Jesus Christ. Through His life, death, and resurrection, Jesus expanded the community of believers to encompass both Jew and Gentile, ushering in a new era of redemption and reconciliation.

Since antiquity, humanity has grappled with the need for moral guidance. The Mosaic Law, originally intended for the well-being of all, became distorted within patriarchal systems, leading to the oppression of women and misunderstanding of divine intent. Yet, amidst this confusion, God's heart remained unchanged, offering liberation and prosperity through His commands.

Ultimately, the covenants of God, rooted in His desire for intimate involvement in human affairs, serve as a beacon of hope, pointing towards the restoration of Eden and the fulfillment of His eschatological promises.

The Patriarchal Framework

In the devout observance of the law, the Jews didn't just adhere to a set of rules; they found solace and connection with the God who bestowed it. Conversely, disobedience weighed heavily on their conscience, casting the law in the harsh light of their own failings.

Understanding the laws of the Old Testament requires delving into the patriarchal framework, where sexuality intertwined with familial dynamics. Picture this: the man as the household's CEO, responsible not just for day-to-day affairs but also for upholding divine law and maintaining familial connections to God.

Within this framework, a woman's sexuality was regarded as the property of her husband, underscoring her role as a bearer of children and reinforcing societal hierarchies. Yet, widowed or divorced women could reclaim ownership of their sexuality, albeit within a society where it remained commodified.

This system, crafted by men post-fall, inherently privileged male dominance, allowing for marital infidelity by men while imposing stringent restrictions on women's sexual autonomy. However, it's essential to recognize that these laws sought to maintain order and protect the vulnerable rather than perpetuate male superiority.

Misnomers and Divine Decrees

Genesis 3:16, often misinterpreted as a divine decree of female subservience, demands deeper scrutiny within its cultural context. It serves as a declaration of the consequences of the fall, rather than a punitive measure against women. To simplify it as justification for female inferiority is to oversimplify its nuanced implications.

To grasp the rationale behind these laws, we must delve into Old Testament culture and customs. Let's journey together through the Scriptures, exploring the intricate tapestry of divine wisdom and human interpretation. By illuminating the relevance of ancient laws to contemporary moral dilemmas, we can bridge the gap between past and present, finding wisdom and guidance for our journey forward.

The translation of the Hebrew word "dia" in the Bible as "for" suggests a common interpretation: that woman was created to meet man's needs, to serve him as a subordinate. Yet, intriguingly, this same word "ezer" is used to describe God as a helper. Does this imply God's subordination to humanity? Rather, it suggests a helper with superior means aiding one with less. Eve likely possessed unique wisdom complementary to Adam's, aiding him in ways he couldn't anticipate. Thus, they formed a complete partnership, each contributing to the household's flourishing.

Genesis doesn't delineate hierarchy between Adam and Eve; she wasn't created to be his servant but his match. Adam's name, derived from "adamah" meaning ground, symbolizes his earthly origins, while Eve's name reflects her creation from Adam's rib, signifying her distinctiveness. Before Eve's arrival, Adam named the animals, signifying his dominance. But her naming post-exile suggests his attempt to dominate her too.

Isn't it striking how women often possess an intuitive insight, perhaps inherited from Eve? Yet, this insight is frequently undervalued, leading to marital conflicts rooted in male dominance. When women's natural abilities are stifled, it breeds resentment and control dynamics, echoing through generations. Sarah's misguided attempt to aid God's plan had lasting repercussions, a cautionary tale against overstepping boundaries.

CHAPTER ONE

God's Imprint on Humanity

It wasn't Adam or Eve's role to fulfill each other's happiness, nor is it God's obligation. Yet, many perceive God's role as ensuring their happiness, leading to disappointment and spiritual struggles. So, why did God create humanity?

At the genesis, God intended to manifest His image spiritually through mankind. Adam's longevity pre-flood and subsequent decline in lifespans underscore humanity's fallen state. Nature's splendor, once abundant, has been marred by catastrophe, irreversibly altered since the flood.

Jesus, as the last Adam, sought to restore humanity's relationship with God and creation. His miraculous conception underscores His divine mission, distinct from ordinary human birth. While the Western world may shy away from such topics, biblical texts hint at encounters with angelic beings, cautioning against spiritual warfare.

By delving into these narratives, we uncover profound truths about humanity's divine purpose and the ongoing struggle for spiritual restoration.

In exploring the divine connection between humanity, the cosmos, and spiritual realms, it's paramount to delve into the intricate relationship between man, earth, and heaven. While hell was designated for the devil, the earth was fashioned as mankind's dwelling, imbued with God's presence.

Before mankind's arrival, a cosmic battle ensued, resulting in Satan's banishment to earth. Nevertheless, the creation of man sparked celestial jubilation, symbolizing a unique bond between humanity and the divine.

Visualize Adam and Eve in their pre-fall state, harmoniously connected to God, radiating spiritual light. In this utopian setting, Satan's deception targeted Eve's compassion and vulnerability, leading to humanity's fall from grace.

The Serpent's Approach

The serpent, once potentially majestic, was cursed to crawl on its belly after deceiving Eve. While evolutionary theories abound, the Genesis narrative suggests divine retribution, stripping the serpent of its limbs as punishment.

Understanding the serpent's approach requires transcending contemporary gender debates and embracing Adam and Eve's primal essence. Adam, symbolizing God's kingly aspect, was created outside the garden, while Eve, fashioned from Adam's flesh within it, represented the soulful dimension. Eve's empathy likely rendered her susceptible to the serpent's subtlety, culminating in humanity's downfall.

It's significant to note that Eve was deceived while Adam knowingly sinned, underscoring their distinct roles in the fall. Interestingly, our Savior entered the world through the flesh of a woman, emphasizing the crucial role of Eve in the redemption narrative. Adam and Eve, together, epitomize the image of God, with Eve positioned alongside Adam rather than beneath him.

God's Foresight

After the fall, death permeated every aspect of existence, and Adam and Eve were expelled from paradise into darkness. Despite this, God foresaw and ultimately resolved humanity's greatest dilemma. As Oswald Chambers aptly puts it, if our problems could be solved by mere mortals, they wouldn't truly be problems. Moreover, biblical psychology underscores humanity's pivotal role in overcoming evil, with God's spirit within man triumphing over the forces of darkness.

"If our problems can be solved by other men, they are not problems at all," says Oswald Chambers in *Baffled to Fight Better*.

And in *Biblical Psychology*, he states, "Man is the climax of creation. He is on a stage a little lower than the angels and God is going to overthrow the devil by this being that is less than angelic. God has, as it were, put man in the open field, and he is allowing the devil to do exactly what he likes up to a certain point, because he says, 'greater is he that is in you, than he that is in the world.' Satan is to be humiliated by man, by the Spirit of God in man through the wonderful regeneration of Jesus Christ.

"Man, then, is the head and the purpose of the six days' creation. Man's body has in it those constituents that connect it with the earth; it has fire and water and all the elements of animal life, consequently, God keeps us here. The earth is man's domain, and we are going to be here again after the terrestrial cremation. 'Here-after,' without the devil, without sin and wrong. We are going to be here, marvelously redeemed in this wonderful place which God made very beautiful, and with which sin has played havoc, and creation itself is waiting for the manifestation of the sons of God."

Chapter One Summary

After years of confusion, I embarked on a journey of discovery, realizing the importance of unraveling the concept of equality rather than allowing its abuses to fester and breed resentment. Reflecting on the creation of Adam and Eve, it becomes evident that they were designed as equals, eliciting awe from celestial observers as they communed with their creator.

In this chapter, we delved into key verses pertaining to the creation of humanity and God's ultimate purpose for mankind. From the genesis of Adam and Eve to the promise of restoration in the New Eden, we traced the trajectory of God's plan through the narrative of creation, fall, and redemption. Understanding these foundational elements allows us to grasp the heart of the Master and his divine intentions manifested through figures like Abraham, Israel, and the Messiah.

Central to God's plan is the desire for intimate involvement in every facet of our lives. By embracing the intricacies of creation, the ramifications of the fall, and the hope of redemption, we align ourselves with the divine purpose, paving the way for a deeper communion with the Creator.

Study questions for chapter one:

1- Who created the system people live by today?

2- Why did a man own a woman's sexuality?

3. What was the purpose of God's law?

4. What was the purpose of God choosing Israel?

5. What are the similarities between Adam and Jesus?

6. Why are Adam and Eve so different?

7. Does God show favor to man or woman?

CHAPTER ONE

Key points from chapter one:

- God had a conceptual idea in creation.
- God's Law was never a means for salvation. It reveals the heart of God toward humankind and his desire for justice.
- God created his law around the standards man had already set, respecting man's free will and ability to think.
- Humanity is God's crowning achievement. Perfect shalom between God and man existed.
- The fall alienated man from God and from one another.
- Early on, man only longed to do evil.
- Man built cities with walls and invented stories of creation through myth.
- God is Sovereign; he had already constructed a master plan to reunite perfect harmony between God and man.
- Israel was meant to be a beacon of truth and hope to the gentiles, not to destroy them.
- Israel's vision turned inward instead of outward.
- Women and children were considered property by men, but not by God.
- God wants to be involved in every aspect of my life.
- The world system was created by men.
- A woman generally did not own her own sexuality.
- Adam named Eve after the fall to dominate her.
- Eve was given a deeper insight to help Adam.
- The image of God in man is spiritual.
- All creation needs salvation after the fall.
- Before the flood man lived 700 years.
- Adam was designed to be eternal.
- From the instant Adam sinned, his union with God died.
- Adam and Jesus were made from the hand of God. All other

men have come from the seed of man.
- The Old Testament foreshadows the Incarnation with an anthropomorphic view of God, that having a body.
- God manifests his spirit in man only by invitation.
- God breathed in man to give him physical life; Jesus breathes into man to give him spiritual life.
- God designed Adam and Eve to stand side by side to make a complete unit, to complement each other.

Closing prayer for chapter one:

"Abba, Thank You for giving me Your law and Your word. Thank You for taking the time to invest in me, Your creation, to protect me. I am thrilled that You want to be so intimately involved in every aspect of my life. Thank You also for giving me the understanding to know Your heart for creating both Adam and Eve. As the years go, may You increase my knowledge of Your word evermore. Write on my heart the truths You want me to remember. Carve them in. I invite You to be manifested in me, and that I may live in a manner worthy of You in all respects. Thank You for giving me clarity and setting me free from the

CHAPTER ONE

deceptions of the world. Amen."

Chapter Two

After the Fall

F*or if we never fell, we should not know how feeble and how wretched we are of our self, and also we should not fully know that marvelous love of our Maker.* —Julian of Norwich

Reflecting on my upbringing near Chicago, I realize how the urban environment and diverse cultural influences shaped my worldview and perceptions of gender roles. From the bustling city streets to the vibrant communities, I encountered a spectrum of experiences that influenced my understanding of identity, relationships, and spirituality.

My journey began amidst the tumult of my parents' divorce,

a pivotal moment that profoundly impacted my upbringing. As a young child, witnessing my father drive away from our home left me grappling with feelings of confusion, abandonment, and loss. This early experience planted seeds of doubt and skepticism about love, family, and faith, shaping my outlook on life in profound ways.

Navigating through life as a woman, I've encountered societal expectations and gender roles that often felt burdensome and confining. From the pressure to fulfill traditional roles as caregiver, homemaker, and nurturer to the constant struggle against stereotypes and biases, the journey of womanhood is fraught with challenges. Yet, amidst these struggles, I've discovered resilience, strength, and a deep sense of purpose in defying expectations and charting my own path.

Reflections on God's Original Design

Contemplating God's original plan for humanity, I am struck by the profound harmony and interconnectedness between spirit, soul, and body. In the Garden of Eden, God fashioned a perfect union between man and creation, intended to reflect His divine image and bring glory to His name. However, the fall from grace fractured this harmony, leading to a distorted understanding of identity, purpose, and relationship with the divine.

As humanity grapples with the consequences of sin, power dynamics and domination have plagued interpersonal relationships and societal structures. From the oppression of women to the exploitation of the vulnerable, the legacy of domination echoes through history, tarnishing the image of God reflected in humanity. Yet, amidst the darkness, there remains a glimmer of hope—a hope rooted in the transformative power of redemption and restoration.

Life in the Garden of Eden: A Glimpse of Paradise

Imagine a lush paradise, meticulously crafted by the hands of God—a sanctuary where Adam and Eve dwelt in perfect harmony with creation. Inside the garden, God's plan unfolded before them, beckoning them to expand its borders and transform the wilderness beyond into a paradise.

In those early days, the world knew no seasons or storms, basking in a perpetual state of tranquility and abundance. God's command to Adam and Eve echoed with purpose: "Be fruitful and multiply, and fill the earth and subdue it." They were royalty, destined to rule over the earth and bring forth its full potential.

Yet, even within the confines of Eden, danger lurked in the form of evil and deception. Satan, embodied in the serpent, sought to corrupt God's perfect creation, leading Adam and Eve astray and casting them out of paradise. However, God's promise of restoration shines brightly on the horizon, as he plans to establish his garden once more during the millennial kingdom, with Jerusalem at its heart—a haven where only the righteous shall dwell.

The Rhythm of Rest and Work: A Divine Example

Reflecting on creation, we see God's intention for rest woven into the fabric of existence—a rhythm between labor and leisure. Adam and Eve were to experience unending Sabbath once they had subdued the earth, basking in the glory of

God's presence. Their nakedness, once a symbol of innocence, became a stark reminder of their fallen state, stripped of the royal garments they were meant to receive.

Adam and Eve's intimacy, once a testament to their unity, shattered in the wake of disobedience. Where once they held each other close, now blame and strife marred their relationship, echoing the struggles of marriages throughout history. Yet, amidst the brokenness, there remains a glimpse of hope—a future union between Christ and his bride, where perfect harmony is restored.

Eden, meaning "pleasure," embodied the essence of God's intention for humanity—to experience joy and fulfillment in communion with Him. Yet, outside the garden, humanity's perception of pleasure has become skewed, leading to the need for divine laws to establish boundaries and guide our paths.

Despite the challenges and trials we face, God's presence remains ever-present, offering solace and hope amidst the chaos. Though some may perceive Him as distant or controlling, His love and compassion endure, leading us towards a future where paradise is restored, and all shall dwell in the pleasure of His presence.

In actuality, he has created the earth with us in mind. For us to enjoy. For our pleasure.

Embracing God's Design

Consider the intricacy of God's design—the gift of five senses bestowed upon humanity. Each sense serves a purpose, not merely for survival, but also for experiencing the richness of creation. From the sight of a sunrise painting the sky with hues of orange and pink to the sound of chirping birds heralding the dawn, every sensory experience reflects God's intention for us to delight in His creation.

Indeed, God crafted the garden not only for sustenance but also for our pleasure. Every aspect of Eden was designed to evoke wonder and joy—a testament to God's attention to detail and His desire for us to experience His goodness.

Yet, amidst the beauty of the garden, the most precious gift was the presence of God Himself. Adam and Eve walked with Him, heard His voice, and gained wisdom and knowledge in His company. However, the shadow of judgment loomed over them, as the commandment not to eat from the tree of knowledge of good and evil filled them with curiosity and apprehension.

Reflecting on the Forbidden Tree: Catalyst for Humanity's Journey

The moment they heard the sound of the LORD God walking in the garden marked the beginning of a new era—a day tinged with fear and uncertainty. Judgment was upon them, and the consequence of disobedience was eviction from the holy land, severing their intimate connection with God.

A glimmer of hope remained—a promise of reunion and restoration foretold in Revelation. Though mankind would face countless trials and battles in the millennia to come, the choice to seek God's presence would remain ever-present, guiding each generation toward redemption.

As we ponder the forbidden tree, let us not view it solely as a symbol of evil, but rather as a catalyst for humanity's journey toward knowledge and understanding. Could Adam and Eve have attained wisdom without partaking of its fruit? Perhaps. Yet, in their disobedience, they embarked on a path fraught with consequences and redemption—a journey woven with the threads of choice and consequence, leading ultimately to reconciliation with their Creator.

This tree provided an eternal opportunity for Adam and Eve to live out their faith. They could have clung to God's goodness and refuted the serpent with the truth. But there was just that little seed of doubt that divided them from the truth. And it wasn't about the existence of God. Rather, they doubted their humanity, believing they could be gods, too.

The head of the serpent could have been crushed once and for all right there. Instead, they rebelled. They lost their royalty. Their position. Their fill of eating from the tree of life. They never needed to experience death, nor did any living thing.

In one instant, everything died, and this became recognizable at once.

Exploring Agrarian Life: Abraham's Society

In the middle section of the book of Genesis, we encounter Abraham, living in an agrarian society where agriculture served as the primary means of sustenance. This lifestyle, deeply rooted in farming and cultivation, shaped the socio-economic fabric of communities and provided the foundation for societal growth and organization.

Agrarian societies relied on agriculture not only for food but also for economic prosperity and social organization. Understanding the intricacies of agrarian life is crucial for comprehending the context in which Abraham and his contemporaries lived and thrived.

The origins of agrarian society predate the first civilizations, emerging alongside early advancements in toolmaking and agriculture. However, societal progress was disrupted by divine judgment, manifesting in catastrophic events like the Great Flood and the confusion of languages.

The shift towards agrarian societies challenged traditional gender roles, leading to the emergence of patriarchal systems where men assumed dominance over women. Despite claims of equality, patriarchal societies perpetuated inequality and subjugation, warranting critical examination and reflection.

While agrarianism prevailed for centuries, the emergence of capitalism in the modern era brought about significant changes in societal structure and values. Capitalism, with its focus on individualism and economic gain, gradually altered familial dynamics and consumption patterns, leading to a shift away from the agrarian way of life.

Capitalism, while initially appearing to advance society, introduced a divide within families and fostered a culture of consumerism and discontent. Transience became prevalent as individuals pursued wealth and material possessions, often at the expense of familial cohesion and connection to the land.

God's Covenant with Abraham: Blessings Tied to the Land

God's covenant with Abraham, promising blessings to his descendants throughout generations, was intimately tied to the land. In an agrarian society, ownership of land was paramount for survival and prosperity. Working the earth and tilling the soil were not only means of sustenance but also acts of worship and obedience to God's commands.

In today's transient society, where land ownership is less common, there is a need to rediscover the sacred connection between humanity and the earth. By understanding the significance of agrarian practices and recognizing the blessings associated with stewardship of the land, we can cultivate a deeper appreciation for God's provision and fulfill our role as caretakers of creation.

Genesis 12:1-3: "Now the LORD said to Abram, 'Go forth from your country, and your relatives and your father's house, to the land which I will show you; And I will make you a great nation, and I will bless you, and make your name great, and so you shall be a blessing; And I will bless those who bless you, and the one who curses you I will curse. And in you, all the families of the earth will be blessed.'"

The above passage magnifies God's heart towards his desire for his people to possess land.

Throughout history, the quest for the Promised Land has been a source of conflict and controversy, with nations vying for control over Israel's territory. Wars and turmoil have plagued the region for millennia, highlighting the enduring significance of Israel and its land in global affairs.

In ancient agrarian societies like Israel, faith in God was paramount. Dependence on divine providence for rain and protection underscored the people's reliance on God's guidance and provision. The prospect of losing land or resorting to slavery was a dire consequence that tested their faith and resilience.

The Emergence of Faith: Abraham's Covenant

Abraham's pivotal role in the history of faith marks the beginning of a covenantal relationship with God. Unlike Adam and Eve, who communed directly with God, Abraham demonstrated faith in the unseen, laying the foundation for a faith-centered covenant with God.

During Abraham's time, amidst a backdrop of idolatry and false worship, his unwavering faith set him apart as a beacon of righteousness. In a society steeped in pagan rituals and human sacrifice, Abraham's devotion to the one true God stood in stark contrast.

Exploring ancestral ties to Judaism and immersing oneself in the artifacts of ancient rituals offer profound insights into the historical context of Abraham's faith journey. Visiting museums like the Israeli Museum in Jerusalem provides a tangible connection to the spiritual heritage passed down through generations.

Abraham's faithfulness laid the groundwork for the chosen nation of God, a testament to divine patience and providence. In a world fraught with corruption and wickedness, God's plan to raise a holy nation reflected His sovereign purpose and unfailing grace.

Evolution of Patriarchy: From Neolithic to Ancient Empires

The transition from the Stone Age to the Neolithic Period marked a significant shift in human society, with the emergence of advanced farming practices leading to the proliferation of patriarchal systems. As civilizations progressed through the Copper, Bronze, and Iron Ages, the roles of men and women underwent profound changes, shaping the social fabric for millennia to come.

The Neolithic culture, originating in modern-day West Bank around 9500 BC, laid the groundwork for sedentary lifestyles and agricultural practices. The cultivation of wild cereals and domestication of animals facilitated settlements and seasonal migrations, laying the foundation for agrarian societies across Asia Minor, North Africa, and North Mesopotamia. However, variations in farming practices emerged due to regional climates and cultural diversity.

Impact of Patriarchy on Ancient Empires

Four major empires—China, India, Mesopotamia, and Egypt—were deeply influenced by patriarchal structures, albeit with distinct nuances and cultural variations.

In China, despite early recognition of female descent rights during the Neolithic period, patriarchal authority strengthened over time. The Shang Dynasty (1766 BC to 1046 BC) witnessed a decline in women's status, epitomized by the practice of foot binding. This painful tradition, endured until the 20th century, symbolized beauty and wealth but inflicted lifelong suffering on women.

The practice of foot binding, prevalent in China for centuries, inflicted lifelong suffering and deformity upon countless women. This painful tradition involved breaking the arch of the foot, gradually reducing its size to a mere three or three and a half inches from toe to heel over a period of about two years. Despite the desired aesthetic of small, delicate feet likened to lotus flowers, foot binding often resulted in serious infections, gangrene, and chronic pain.

Bound feet symbolized wealth and status, as women with small feet were exempt from manual labor and could afford to hire slaves. The Lotus Gait, characterized by a seductive sway, was considered appealing to men and became associated with femininity and desirability. Originating from the deformed feet of an emperor's daughter, foot binding became synonymous with royalty and social prestige.

Contemporary Gender Challenges

Despite efforts to eradicate harmful practices like foot binding, modern China grapples with deep-rooted gender disparities and systemic injustices. Poor families resort to selling daughters into prostitution or as mail-order brides, perpetuating cycles of exploitation and abuse. Policies such as forced abortion and the one-child maximum exacerbate gender-based discrimination, leading to a disproportionate number of female suicides. The alarming rate of female suicide, surpassing that of men, highlights the urgent need for gender equality and mental health support initiatives. The situation so dark, more women commit suicide in China than men, the only place in the world where this is recorded. Every four minutes a woman attempts to take her life and succeeds.

Caste System and Patriarchy in Ancient India

In ancient India, adherence to the Lawbook of Manu governed gender roles, emphasizing honor and respect for women within the patriarchal hierarchy. Women were expected to fulfill traditional roles as wives and mothers, subject to the authority of their fathers, husbands, or sons. The primary measure of a woman's worth lay in her ability to bear children and manage the household.

Ancient India was marked by a rigid caste system that entrenched social hierarchies and gender inequalities. Alongside patriarchy, which relegated women to subordinate roles, the caste system further stratified society based on occupation and birth. The hierarchical order, from highest to lowest, included priests, warriors, merchants, peasants, and untouchables, with individuals confined to their caste for life.

The practice of suttee, or sati, epitomized the devaluation of women in ancient Indian society. When an elite man died, his wife was expected to immolate herself on his funeral pyre as an act of devotion. Despite attempts to portray suttee as voluntary, many instances involved coercion, often facilitated by opium consumption followed by forced immolation. Widows who refused suttee faced ostracism from society and relied on others' charity for survival, regardless of their age or circumstances.

While suttee remains practiced among orthodox Hindus today, it is widely condemned as a human rights violation. Other contentious issues in Indian culture, such as polygamy, widows' rights to remarry, divorce, and women's education, have come under scrutiny amid Western cultural influences, notably facilitated by the internet. These debates reflect ongoing efforts to challenge traditional norms and promote gender equality and social justice in Indian society.

Hammurabi's Code in Mesopotamia

Hammurabi's Code, consisting of 282 written laws, exemplified the patriarchal structure of Mesopotamian society. Hammurabi, a Babylonian king reigning from approximately 1796 BC to 1750 BC, claimed divine authority for the establishment of his laws, declaring himself chosen by the gods to bring about righteousness in the land.

In Mesopotamian culture, men held higher status than

women, with key decisions and responsibilities vested in male authority figures. Men were primarily responsible for tasks such as allocating work within the family and arranging marriages for their children and dependents. While elite women might wield influence in matters of kingship and governance, particularly within royal courts, ordinary women lacked individual agency and typically operated in support of their fathers or husbands.

Marriages in Mesopotamia, as in other ancient civilizations, were often arranged and typically occurred after puberty. Upon engagement, a woman became part of her future husband's family, and in the event of his death, she might be betrothed to one of his brothers or male relatives. This practice reinforced familial ties and ensured the continuity of inheritance and social structures within patriarchal society.

Gender Equality in Ancient Egypt

In ancient Egypt, despite the prevailing patriarchal structure, women of royalty enjoyed elevated status and rights that surpassed those of women in many contemporary cultures. Unlike in other societies, where gender often determined social standing, in Egypt, class distinctions were more prominent, leading to a greater degree of equality between men and women.

Women in ancient Egypt possessed legal rights that allowed them to manage and own private property, engage in legal disputes, and participate in marital and familial affairs without the need for male representation. They could initiate divorces, sue, free slaves, and exercise control over inheritance and property division.

Marriage in ancient Egypt was viewed as a duty, with girls typically marrying around the age of fourteen. Unlike modern ceremonies, Egyptian weddings lacked formal rituals or ceremonies; a girl simply left her parents' home to join her husband's household. While men were permitted to have multiple wives, incest was prohibited except among royalty.

Women in ancient Egypt retained property rights throughout their lives, owning everything they possessed before, during, and after marriage. In the event of a divorce or the death of a husband, women retained one-third of the property, with the remainder allocated to children or other relatives. Additionally, women had the freedom to distribute inheritance as they saw fit among their offspring.

Unlike in some contemporary societies, women in ancient Egypt enjoyed relative freedom of movement in public spaces. They were not confined to the domestic sphere and could engage in various activities outside the home.

As in other ancient societies, the value of both men and women in ancient Egypt was often associated with their ability to bear children. The number of offspring a woman bore contributed significantly to her social status and perceived value within the community.

Religion and Patriarchy in Ancient Societies

Religion played a significant role in shaping patriarchal systems across various ancient cultures, though the specific beliefs and practices varied from region to region.

In ancient Israel, monotheism was the prevailing religious belief, with a focus on the worship of a single deity. This monotheistic tradition contributed to the unique character of

Israel's patriarchal society.

Confucianism emerged as the dominant religious and philosophical influence in China, emphasizing morality and social order. Emperors were revered as divine beings, reinforcing hierarchical structures within society.

Hinduism, with its complex pantheon of gods and goddesses, provided a framework of strict moral and social codes governing behavior. The caste system further reinforced social hierarchies and patriarchal norms.

Mesopotamian society was polytheistic, with each city-state worshiping its own set of deities. Rituals, sacrifices, and divination played integral roles in religious practice, contributing to the overarching patriarchal structure.

Egyptian religion was characterized by mythological narratives and the worship of pharaohs as divine incarnations. Pharaonic authority was central to societal organization, perpetuating patriarchal ideals.

Debates on Matriarchy

While some historians suggest the existence of matriarchal societies, conclusive evidence remains elusive. The term "matrifocal" is sometimes used to describe social structures where maternal figures hold prominence, emphasizing the essential role of women in nurturing and sustaining life.

Matrifocal societies recognize women as the primary caregivers and nurturers, acknowledging their indispensable role in the survival and well-being of communities. This acknowledgment reflects a God-designed order where women serve as the source of life and nurturing within society.

CHAPTER TWO

The Hebrew Family and Social Structure

In the Levant, the state of Israel stood apart from previous empires, living as monotheists. The Hebrew family served as both a social foundation and a business entity. Families were organized into clans, which then combined to form tribes. The early Hebrews operated under a matriarchal system, where kinship was determined by the maternal lineage. This meant that individuals born to Jewish mothers were considered Jewish, regardless of their father's ethnicity.

Contrary to common assumptions, women in Hebrew society held significant roles and status. Figures like Sarah, Rebecca, Rachel, Miriam, Rahab, Deborah, Esther, and Ruth exemplify the diverse duties and responsibilities undertaken by women. While women were involved in physically demanding tasks such as tent pitching and fieldwork, the male head of the household retained authority over certain religious and ceremonial duties, reinforcing male domination.

Evolution of Patriarchal Societies

Over time, agrarian societies witnessed a diminishing importance of women's roles and status. Despite societal advancements from the Neolithic to historic times, the fundamental roles of women in childbearing and household management remained constant. The increasing demands of societal sophistication placed additional burdens on women, leading to physical strain and poorer health.

Patriarchal societies imposed codes that restricted women's autonomy and decision-making authority. Women were expected to be supportive and obedient to the male head of the family, known as the paterfamilias. This dynamic was reinforced by the custom of women leaving their families to join their husband's household, often including his parents. This adjustment posed challenges for women, requiring them to assimilate into unfamiliar familial structures.

Critics argue that traditional customs, such as the woman leaving her family to join her husband's household, are outdated. Drawing from Genesis, some propose an alternative where the man leaves his family to join the woman's household, allowing her to maintain familiarity and continuity within her own family structure.

By gaining insight into historical customs and societal structures, women can navigate contemporary challenges more effectively. Understanding one's position under God's master plan provides a foundation for progress and empowerment, rooted in the principles established from the beginning of time.

In the next chapter, we will take a closer look at patriarchy.

Chapter Two Summary

In exploring the main four empires of antiquity and the unique foundation of life in ancient Israel, the solitary monotheistic nation of its time, one cannot overlook the challenges faced by women during this era. Each empire presented its own set of hurdles, painting a diverse picture of ancient lifestyles vastly different from our contemporary norms.

The stark disparities between ancient and modern life serve as a poignant reminder to appreciate the advancements of civilization. Reviewing these historical epochs instills a sense of gratitude for the conveniences and opportunities afforded to women today. The nineteenth and twentieth centuries, in particular, witnessed groundbreaking inventions that significantly eased the burdens of traditional female roles.

Today, women enjoy a breadth of experiences beyond traditional domestic duties, relishing the freedom to pursue diverse interests and activities. From academic pursuits to creative endeavors, modern conveniences empower women to engage in leisurely pursuits such as music, exploration, and relaxation by the seaside.

While modern life offers liberation from the confines of antiquated roles, it's essential to remember the arduous labor endured by women in ancient times. Tasks like spinning, once vital for daily existence, required constant effort and ingenuity, evidenced by the development of various spinning wheel designs tailored to different contexts, including portable options for nomadic lifestyles.

Chapter Two illuminates the transformative impact of the expulsion from Eden on the roles of men and women, emphasizing the centrality of land ownership in ancient societies. Furthermore, the exploration of Mosaic Law unveils its underlying purpose: the nurturing and protection of a nascent nation chosen by God. As we delve deeper into the heart of divine law, we glimpse the profound care and guidance of the Creator towards his people.

Study questions for chapter two:

1. How did the four empires differ from each other and how are they the same today for women?

2. Why is faith first associated with Abraham?

3. When and why did man's importance escalate?

4. Why is it said that without the care of a woman a man could not live?

5. What might the challenges or dangers have been for a woman living in a monotheistic state amidst other states that were practicing polytheism?

6. How does knowing all of this help to set one free?

7. How can one apply it in relationships?

Key points from chapter two:

- Most people live as if they can reach the highest good in themself, by themself.
- An agrarian society is one that lives off the land for its sustenance.
- Without land in antiquity, survival was difficult.
- Faith is first associated with Abraham.
- The first civilization began in Sumer, Mesopotamia.
- Cities were a place of darkness and evil deeds.
- Patriarchy had its origins in Sumer.
- Man was already advanced in knowledge and had built the Tower of Babel.
- Women were doing the bulk of the work.
- Man's importance escalated as times changed and moved into the period known as the Iron Age.
- Four empires existed: China, India, Egypt, and Mesopotamia
- Today life is so grim for women in China that every four

CHAPTER TWO

minutes a woman commits suicide.
- In India, the value of a woman is diminished by sati practices.
- In antiquity, women from Egypt had more rights than in other cultures.
- Only the state of Israel was monotheistic.
- Without the many stages of a woman's care, men would not survive.
- Women in Israel were more respected than in other cultures.
- Women were physically weakened by childbearing and strained from their many duties.

Closing prayer for chapter two:

"Abba, Thank You for teaching me about the different cultures in antiquity. And thank You for calling Abraham to Yourself, setting him apart to build a chosen people. Thank You for revealing Yourself to me. I also want to give thanks for all the ways You have helped to release a woman to live more abundantly and to have more leisure time. I pray You can guide me where and when to apply all that I am learning. I hold no grudges in my heart and pray that if I ever do, You will reveal them to me so I may be rid of them. I desire to walk in integrity, always. Though my heart and my flesh may fail, You are the joy of my heart and my strength forever. Amen."

Chapter Three

Patriarchy

W<i>hat hast Thou taught me, O, Love Uncreated? Thou hast taught me that I should bear patiently like a lamb, not only harsh words, but even blows harsh and hard, and injury and loss.</i> —St. Catherine of Siena

In contemplating the complexities of relationships and marriage, it's evident that societal attitudes and structures significantly influence our perceptions and behaviors. In recent years, I've observed a pervasive sense of selfishness and misguided priorities, leading me to question why we struggle to navigate these fundamental aspects of human connection. At times, I've found myself nostalgically reflecting on ancient practices such as arranged marriages and communal living, wondering if they offered a more stable foundation for partnership and family life.

Reflections on Relationships and Marriage

Marriage customs varied widely across different cultures, but a common thread emerged in the early institution of arranged marriages and contractual agreements. While initially designed to protect women from mistreatment, these laws often reinforced their subordinate status within society. Polygamy was commonplace among men, particularly among the wealthy elite, while women were bound by strict societal expectations and limited freedoms.

Social stratification further exacerbated gender disparities, with visible distinctions between the roles of men and women in upper-class versus peasant societies. Wealthy women were often relegated to ornamental roles, devoid of the physical labor that characterized the lives of their lower-class counterparts. The silence and submission expected of women in elite circles contrasted sharply with the vocal assertiveness of those who defied societal norms, forming networks and support systems to navigate their constrained realities.

The Grim Reality of Infanticide

Perhaps the most distressing manifestation of gender inequality was the practice of infanticide, particularly in response to fears of overpopulation. Male infants were often spared to ensure the continuation of family lines, highlighting the dire consequences of patriarchal power dynamics and the systemic devaluation of female lives.

Yet when overpopulation was feared, girls would be victims of infanticide by their parents. Throughout the Roman Empire, China, Japan, and India this was a common practice and girls were particularly vulnerable. Infanticide was actually encouraged in antiquity. And its practice was quite gruesome. The grim fate awaiting unwanted infants further underscores the stark reality of a patriarchal society where children, particularly female infants, were often regarded as expendable commodities. In a world where male dominance reigned supreme, the lives of children held little value compared to the preservation of patriarchal power structures.

Infants who escaped the tragic fate of infanticide were still vulnerable to other forms of exploitation, such as being sold into slavery or sacrificed in rituals to appease deities. These harrowing practices highlight the callous disregard for the sanctity of life and the pervasive grip of patriarchal norms on every aspect of society.

In contrast to the value placed on children in contemporary times, where their well-being and rights are championed, ancient societies operated under a vastly different ethos. Children were viewed through the lens of utility and lineage preservation, with little consideration for their inherent worth as human beings. Such stark disparities serve as a sobering reminder of the progress made in recognizing and safeguarding the rights of children in modern society.

Unveiling the Mystery of Patriarchy

Unraveling the enigma of patriarchy and its role in divine governance has been a journey of enlightenment. Initially perplexed by God's incorporation of patriarchal structures and laws, my understanding evolved as I delved into historical contexts and societal dynamics.

Defined by the Oxford dictionary as a system where male dominance prevails, patriarchy governed societies worldwide during the era of Mosaic Law. However, contrary to popular belief, patriarchy did not originate from divine decree but was rather a prevalent social construct.

God's interaction within patriarchal frameworks was akin to a wise father reinforcing his child's creation. Rather than abolishing existing systems, God worked within them, providing guidance and stability while respecting human agency.

Within Jewish worship, the priest symbolized the patriarchal head of the household, leading sacrificial rituals and serving as a conduit for divine communication. Despite patriarchal structures, God communicated with his people through various channels, illustrating his ongoing engagement. God was then communicating to his people by dreams, visions, appearances, and ambassadors like Melchizedek. Adam, Job, Noah, Abraham, Isaac, Jacob, and others illustrate patriarchal worship of God.

Israel stood apart as God's chosen people, separated from the surrounding Gentile nations governed by their own patriarchal laws and idolatrous practices. God's covenant with Israel underscored his commitment to a people set apart for his purpose. Separated from the rest of the known world, the Israelites were God's chosen and holy people for his own possession. Until the Gentile nations were presented the gospel, they continued under rigid Patriarchal Law and idolatry, living completely separated from their Creator.

Reflecting on Patriarchy: A Journey of Understanding

This exploration invites reflection on the intersection of divine sovereignty and human agency within patriarchal systems. By understanding God's intervention within societal norms, we gain deeper insights into the complexities of divine governance and human relationships.

Two major laws are revealed to the chosen people in the Old Testament. During the times of Patriarchal Law, the father or head of the household in Israel spoke to God to distinguish God's will and guidance concerning the household. Starting with Abraham, in an agrarian society, this law prevailed until the Mosaic Law was initiated. It is thought to have lasted around twenty-five hundred years.

Mosaic Law began as a result of the burning bush and God speaking to Moses, thus delivering his chosen people from bondage, and establishing the Ten Commandments along with the Sundry and Levitical Laws about moral, physical, and spiritual welfare. This law extended over a period of fifteen hundred years until Christ came and fulfilled it.

God's Design for His Chosen People

Throughout history, God's chosen ones have been called to live set apart for Him, embodying a deep intimacy with their Creator. However, as time progressed and technology advanced, society drifted further from this fundamental truth, leading to the gradual diminishment of women's worth and a sense of being taken for granted.

Contrary to a chaotic compilation of laws and facts, the Pentateuch intricately lays out God's blueprint for birthing a nation set apart. From civil acts to acts of worship, Israel's distinctiveness was evident through its exceptional laws of hygiene and worship, setting it apart from surrounding cultures.

Polygamy, common in patriarchal societies, found its place within Mosaic Law but with stricter regulations. Marrying close relatives was customary until the time of Abraham, emphasizing the significance of family and clan bonds in Israelite society.

In certain cases, women opted for marriages outside their clan, known as Sadiqa marriages, provided their children remained subordinate to their clan and appropriate compensation was offered. Examples like Gideon and Samson in the book of Judges shed light on the acceptance and prevalence of this practice among the Hebrews.

The tribe of Levi, entrusted with the care of the tabernacle, faced prohibitions against marrying foreigners, reflecting God's desire to maintain spiritual purity within Israel. Similarly, marrying individuals from specific Canaanite nations was forbidden due to their depravity and undesirable spiritual influence.

Unveiling the Dynamics of Marriage in Mosaic Law

In Hebrew culture, the distinction between betrothal and marriage was clear, marking the commencement of a lifelong bond. Betrothal, a formal transaction between parents and close family friends, involved the negotiation of a dowry and required the bride's consent. Once sealed, the marriage was consummated, symbolizing the union's finality.

The wedding process in Hebrew culture held profound symbolism, mirroring Christ's love for his bride, the church. The groom's preparation of a place in his father's house echoed Jesus' promise to prepare a place for his disciples. The bride, adorned and pure, awaited her groom's arrival, reminiscent of the church's anticipation of Christ's return.

Marriage vows in Mosaic Law reflected the sacred covenant between God and his chosen people. Divorce and remarriage were prohibited, emphasizing the eternal nature of God's love and commitment to his bride. The symbolism behind these laws highlights the profound spiritual truths embedded in Hebrew marital customs.

In cases of marital transgression, the purification ritual served as a symbolic means of purging evil from the family name. The woman accused of adultery underwent a rigorous test, consuming a potion mixed with temple dust. This ritual, shrouded in controversy, aimed to uphold purity and restore social order within Hebrew society.

Reflecting on ancient practices, such as purification rituals and early marriage contracts, can be challenging given the stark differences from contemporary society. The transformative message of Jesus, however, ushered in new understandings and societal norms, reshaping attitudes towards marriage and adultery.

Evolution of Social Standards

Over time, societal attitudes towards adultery evolved, with rabbis expanding the definition to include husbands' infidelity. The influence of early Christianity, particularly the teachings of Christ, played a significant role in shaping these shifting social norms.

In ancient times, marriage contracts were often arranged for girls as young as twelve or fourteen, marking the beginning of their marital journey. Upon marriage, girls would transition to their husband's household, joining the work and care provided by older women in the family.

While ancient customs may seem foreign to contemporary sensibilities, understanding the historical context helps bridge the gap between past practices and modern perspectives on marriage and relationships. Through reflection and awareness, we can appreciate the progress made while acknowledging the complexities of our shared human experience across time.

In ancient societies, early marriage was common, driven by the desire for children and societal perceptions of puberty. Girls were often married off soon after reaching puberty, as virginity was highly valued, and there were fears surrounding menstruation.

Marriage ceremonies were elaborate affairs, with the bridegroom adorned as a king and crowned. He would ceremoniously take the veiled bride from her father's house amidst celebrations that lasted for seven days. These rituals held deep symbolism, often reflecting themes of royalty and anticipation akin to the Second Coming.

Divorce was prevalent among the Israelites, often stemming from issues like barrenness or perceived unseemliness. Wealthy childless women could offer their maidservants to their husbands to avoid divorce. Additionally, concubinage was common, with concubines occupying a socially and domestically inferior status, yet their children were considered legitimate.

Despite the prevalence of divorce, women lacked the right to separate from their husbands, even in cases of adultery. Adulterous husbands faced severe consequences, including stoning. Women were entitled to legal support, but some men sought divorce to evade financial obligations, while others turned to prostitution, which later became unlawful in Hebrew culture.

Hebrew Family Dynamics and Social Structure

In Hebrew society, families led simple, frugal lives, prioritizing necessity over leisure. Activities like fishing and hunting weren't seen as sport but as essential for survival. Unique codes governed slavery, with Mosaic Law prohibiting involuntary servitude or selling of slaves. Hebrew slaves were entitled to freedom after a designated term, while mistreatment of maidservants led to their emancipation.

Hebrew society revolved around the bayit (house) and bet ab (father's house), forming subtribes, tribes, and eventually the nation. This tribal structure tightly bound individuals within a social framework, emphasizing family units and reputations. The covenant between God and Israel began at the tribal level, permeating through households to individuals.

The Fifth Commandment elevated the family to a holy status, second only to the Temple, underscoring its importance in Jewish society. Patriarchal families served as economic and political organizations, providing a robust social order that rendered the state nearly unnecessary, particularly outside of wartime.

Like other agrarian societies, large families were crucial in ancient Israel for sustaining the family business, caring for aging parents, and preserving the family name. Males wielded control over property, possessions, and wealth, and sons were preferred due to their physical strength and role in perpetuating the family lineage.

In ancient Israel, children were considered the property of the father, placing ultimate responsibility on him for their well-being. In cases of seduction or false accusations against daughters, the father was compensated. Additionally, he had the authority to sell his daughter as a slave, handmaid, concubine, or pledge his son's services as a loan guarantee.

The patriarch of the family, typically the oldest male, held governing authority. A culture of respect for aged males prevailed, with the oldest son often acting on behalf of the father. Marriages for daughters were arranged based on their age, with the eldest marrying first, although exceptions occurred due to the influence of the wife's power within the household.

Mosaic Law included provisions aimed at protecting tribal unity and individual harmony within families. Severe penalties, such as the death sentence, were imposed on children who disobeyed the commandment to honor their parents.

To prevent conflicts and rivalries within families, laws prohibited sisters from marrying the same husband and forbade incestuous relationships. The integrity of the entire tribe or subtribe could be jeopardized by the actions of a single family unit, underscoring the importance of these laws in preserving social cohesion. In the following chapter, we delve into some of these laws in more detail.

Chapter Three Summary

Studying the customs and daily life of antiquity has been a fascinating journey. In Jewish society, the tribes, clans, and families were the focal points, each member contributing to the common good. Marriages were strategic alliances aimed at strengthening families rather than romantic unions.

Patriarchy was deeply entrenched, with the head of the household acting as the intermediary between the family and God. Marriage contracts were designed for the benefit of the household, and weddings were rich in symbolism, anticipating Christ's return for his bride.

Divorcing a barren woman was common, and prostitution was legal. Hygiene laws in Israel differed from those of neighboring cultures. With high mortality rates and a life expectancy of around 40 years, survival was precarious. Furthermore, independence was unthinkable within Israel without the support of one's subtribe.

Study questions for chapter three:

1. Why didn't God intrude on the system and codes set by men?

2. What was good about the daily life of Jews in antiquity?

3. Is there anything that would benefit society if still present in today's culture?

4. Is daily life today for most believers set apart for God like it was for those under Mosaic Law?

5. How was daily life different in Israel than in its surrounding nations?

6. How was the Jewish wedding ceremony symbolic?

7. Is there anything one can do presently to help children better cope with the challenges life brings them?

Key points from chapter three:

- Prostitution was lawful in antiquity.
- Women found guilty of adultery were put to death. Men were treated more lightly, except under Mosaic Law.
- The physical difference between people of different classes was evident.
- Until the Gentile nations were presented the gospel, they continued under rigid Patriarchal Law.
- God did not intrude in the law that man had set in his world, but he set Mosaic Law to protect the innocent.
- A proper Jewish head of the house would inquire God for his guidance within the household.
- The daily life of God's chosen people has always been directed to be set apart for him.
- With its outstanding laws of hygiene and worship, Israel was visibly different than all of the other cultures that surrounded it.
- Betrothal was a business in Israel and only considered legal upon the daughter's consent.
- The Jewish wedding ceremony is spiritually symbolic.
- The average life expectancy in antiquity was around 40.
- People believed once puberty began, girls were craving

impregnation and it was urgent to marry them off.
- Divorce was common.
- Many men divorced to avoid having to support barren women.
- Israel was made of up tribes and subtribes which were tightly structured. No one could exist independently.
- It was essential to have large families.
- Daughters were married by age rank.

Closing prayer for chapter three:

"Abba, I come to You with a humble spirit. Forgive me if I have not been living my daily life set apart for You. I know You care for me and want me to involve You in every area of my life. Thank You for so carefully calling one nation to be set apart for You, and for training the people in the way they should go. I appreciate all the symbolism You shared with Your children. How their marriage ceremony is the most special in the world. I look forward to how You will return to claim Your bride. May You make her ready. While I wait for You, please continue to strengthen me and to impart more wisdom upon me. Please give all parents the knowledge and urgency to help their children cope in the real world. For it is indeed a cruel one.

Amen."

Chapter Four

Beginning to Understand the Beginning

L*ife appears to me to be too short to be spent in nursing animosity or registering wrong.* —Charlotte Brontë

Before delving into an in-depth study of Mosaic Law, I struggled to reconcile God's assertion of equality between men and women with the apparent male favoritism in the law. The disparity seemed glaring, especially in societal roles where women were relegated to supporting roles in the church and elsewhere.

However, I realized that there must be more to the story, prompting me to embark on a journey of exploration and understanding. This journey has been anything but painful;

it has been enlightening and full of promise. As I began to contextualize the societal norms of antiquity and understand the roots of male dominance, a new perspective emerged.

It became clear that God was working within the framework established by men, and understanding this context was crucial to grasping the deeper truths within Mosaic Law. This realization marked the beginning of a paradigm shift in my thinking, one that continues to shape my understanding of gender equality in the eyes of God. In fact, I think it's something every woman should know.

God's Framework Through Mosaic Law

As we delve into specific verses, you will need your Bible to follow along. In this section on Mosaic Law, I'm not unpacking the whole law, rather pulling out those complicated laws involving women with a lens focusing on equality.

In Exodus 21-23, focusing on property rights, personal care, and various laws, it becomes evident that God's directives aim to address the dangers of domination, particularly by men. The responsibilities and penalties outlined in these laws underscore the principle of accountability for both genders.

For instance, consider the treatment of male and female slaves in Exodus 21:1-11. While both are subject to servitude, there are significant differences in their terms of service. Male slaves are granted freedom after six years, but if they choose to remain in service, they undergo a symbolic act of "sealing" by their master. This sealing represents a commitment to continued service, akin to the spiritual sealing of believers by God.

By examining such laws closely, we begin to uncover the

underlying principles of justice and fairness that underpin Mosaic Law, challenging the notion of male dominance and highlighting the shared accountability of both men and women before God.

Symbolism and Equality in Mosaic Law

The treatment of single female slaves in Mosaic Law differs from that of male slaves, yet it holds symbolic significance. While male slaves have the choice to go free after a period of service, female slaves are set free only by default or if rejected by their master. This may seem unequal, but it serves to protect them from potential destitution without a husband to support them. Additionally, the law stipulates that if the female slave is redeemed, she must be treated as an heir or daughter, ensuring her dignity and protection within the household.

This symbolism reflects the redemption and care provided by Christ to his chosen bride, highlighting the sacredness and significance of the relationship between husband and wife. Furthermore, the severe punishment for striking one's parents underscores the importance of honoring and revering both parents equally, emphasizing the sacred union and authority shared by married couples.

Divine Protection for Women and the Innocent

In verses 22-27, we witness God's profound concern for the sanctity of life and justice, especially regarding women and the vulnerable.

In verse 22, the severity of the punishment underscores the value of life itself. The principle of "eye for an eye" serves as a guideline for justice, ensuring that those who cause harm face appropriate consequences. This principle extends to protect unborn life, as seen in the case of harming a pregnant woman.

God's law extends to protect even slaves from unjust harm. If a master injures a slave, resulting in the loss of an eye or tooth, the slave is to be set free. This provision highlights God's concern for the well-being of all individuals, regardless of their social status.

Verses 16-18 emphasize the importance of a woman's virginity and dignity. If a man seduces a virgin, he is obligated to marry her and provide for her, respecting her rights and dignity. This law safeguards women's honor and ensures that they are not taken advantage of or left vulnerable.

Verse 22 reinforces God's protection for widows and orphans, who were particularly vulnerable in ancient society. By prohibiting the affliction of widows and orphans, God ensures that the vulnerable are not exploited or mistreated, holding society accountable for their well-being.

Divine Justice and Protection

In verses 23-24, God's promise to hear the cries of the afflicted and mete out justice underscores his commitment to protecting the vulnerable. Those who oppress others face divine retribution, with their families suffering the consequences of their actions.

Reflecting on the moral clarity of Mosaic Law, the author expresses a yearning for the values it upholds, contrasting it with the moral ambiguity of modern society. Finding solace in the love of God, they recognize the profound impact of experiencing divine love for the first time.

Chapter twenty-three delves into the symbolism of Sabbath and land laws, drawing parallels between the restorative cycles of creation and the anticipated return of Christ. These laws are seen as intricately woven into the fabric of time, reflecting God's grand design for humanity.

Notably, Mosaic Law does not treat women and children as property, affirming their intrinsic worth and dignity. Despite the seriousness of these laws, they serve as a testament to God's impartiality and concern for the vulnerable.

The author contends that God views women as equals to men, emphasizing their complementary roles in forming a unified whole. Drawing parallels between human relationships and the divine Trinity, they highlight the importance of mutual love and respect between genders.

In fact, there's no way for them to be unequal. It's not possible. Nor is it possible for a man and a woman to be unequal. It wasn't until God made the woman that he called his creation very good. Until she was made, the entire universe was incomplete!

Recognize what Paul said about the Mosaic Law in Romans 5:20, "The Law came in so that the transgression would increase; but where sin increased, grace abounded all the more." It became necessary for the Israelites to identify with their sin, their nature that separated them from God and to begin to make restitution and to atone for it. Paul wasn't talking about their sins.

In Paul's discourse, he addresses the pervasive nature of sin inherited from Adam and contrasts it with the abundance of grace made available through Christ. He highlights how grace, like a superior law, transcends and overcomes the law of sin.

Drawing an analogy between physical laws, I illustrate how

grace operates as a higher principle, akin to the law of buoyancy superseding gravity. Just as one must immerse themselves in water to be free from gravity's pull, embracing grace is essential to liberation from the law of sin.

Merely acknowledging the existence of the law is insufficient; one must actively embrace grace to experience true freedom from the bondage of sin. Like stepping into water, stepping into grace is the decisive action that leads to liberation from the law's grip.

Examining Domestic Relations in Deuteronomy

Deuteronomy offers further insights into God's laws, illustrating his fervent protection and purpose for Israel. These laws serve as additional safeguards as the nation grows in number. At this point, it would be good to read Deuteronomy 21 to really study what it is saying regarding domestic relations.

One notable command is the directive to treat a slandered bride with justice, emphasizing God's concern for fairness and dignity even in marital disputes.

In a striking move, God shifts the judgment of an adulterous wife from the violated husband to the public, underscoring the severity of the offense and the communal responsibility for upholding moral standards.

Deuteronomy also addresses the treatment of captive women, highlighting God's compassion even for those in vulnerable positions. The severity of punishment for mistreating a captive woman underscores the gravity of sexual abuse and the sanctity of human dignity.

Reflecting on these laws prompts contemplation of their relevance in contemporary society. In particular, the contrast between the punishment for rape under Mosaic Law and its treatment in modern culture raises important questions about justice and societal values.

This author shares personal insights, drawing from their own experiences with sexual assault and the societal challenges victims often face. My firsthand encounter underscores the enduring importance of addressing sexual violence with seriousness and compassion.

Deuteronomy's Lessons

Deuteronomy's laws offer valuable lessons about justice, compassion, and the sanctity of human dignity. They serve as a reminder of God's unwavering commitment to protecting his people and upholding moral standards, challenging us to consider how these principles apply in our own lives and societies.

I would like to reference verses twelve and thirteen regarding taking a captive for a wife. Why does this captive have to cut her hair, trim her nails, and remove her clothes? Is she detestable to God? Is her body detestable to God? Maybe.

In these verses, God mandates specific hygiene practices for a captive woman taken as a wife. While some may interpret this as a reflection of her being detestable to God, it's more likely a practical measure rooted in hygiene. In antiquity, only the Jewish state practiced good hygiene, and these steps would have been crucial for cleansing the body from bacteria. By mandating these practices, God ensures the well-being of both the captive woman and the rest of the tribe, emphasizing his concern for hygiene and health.

In verses 15-17, God commands fathers to honor the

birthright of the firstborn, symbolizing the importance of preserving lineage and avoiding conflicts such as Jacob's usurpation of Esau's birthright. This law serves both practical and symbolic purposes, promoting peace and order within families and communities.

Verses 18-21 are concerned with the rebellious son. While some may question the fairness of this law, it's essential to understand the context of ancient society. In a patriarchal culture where disobedience was severely punished, God's command regarding a rebellious son reflects the need for order and respect within the family unit. The absence of rebellious daughters in this context likely stems from societal norms where females, children, and slaves had limited options and were expected to adhere to authority without question. They, in essence, didn't possess the freewill of sons.

Today, definitions of unruly behavior may differ significantly, with societal attitudes toward activities like binge drinking often normalized or even celebrated. This societal shift underscores the importance of addressing issues of disobedience and parental authority in modern contexts, highlighting the ongoing relevance of principles of respect and accountability within families.

Understanding Cultural Context: Deuteronomy 22

In Deuteronomy 22, we encounter a range of laws and moral guidelines that may seem perplexing to modern readers but were significant in the cultural and societal context of the time. Each law served a specific purpose, promoting order, morality, and care within the community.

One particularly challenging passage, Deuteronomy 22:13-21,

addresses the issue of blood on the sheets after consummation and its significance in ancient customs. While this may seem crude to contemporary sensibilities, it reflects common practices of the time, where the presence of blood signified the bride's virginity and the integrity of the marriage contract.

Blood rites were significant moments in a woman's life in ancient cultures, marking milestones such as menstruation, the wedding night, and childbirth. These rites symbolized the value placed on a woman's ability to bear children and maintain her family's lineage.

Before the wedding night, brides underwent extensive preparation, including learning domestic skills and ensuring a substantial bride price to enhance their status and rank in society. The bloody sheet served as tangible proof of the bride's virginity and the honesty of the dowry exchange.

Childbirth, the culmination of a woman's preparation and purpose, was celebrated as a significant achievement, particularly if the child was a son, bringing increased status to the family. However, it's essential to recognize the inherent inequality and societal pressures surrounding childbirth and gender roles in ancient times.

While childbirth is a common occurrence today, it remains a miraculous and awe-inspiring event. Understanding the cultural and historical context helps us appreciate the significance of these rites and rituals, even as we recognize the need for progress and equality in our modern understanding of gender and family dynamics.

Each stage was a defined phase in the life of a developing woman into a new role. At the onset of menstruation, a girl becomes a woman. At marriage, a woman becomes a wife upon losing her virginity. And upon bearing a child, a woman becomes a mother. All of these bring celebration, defined rules, and expectations. And all of these require the shedding of blood.

I do not think it is the central purpose of a woman's life. I think it is the central achievement. A crown on her head. But I do not think a woman is incomplete for not bearing children. I think her highest purpose is to seek God and to know him. Sometimes, children can disturb and interrupt this process. Yet a woman glorifies God and worships him without knowing it as she raises her children if she rears them in the complete knowledge of him.

Understanding Ancient Laws: Protection and Societal Dynamics

In examining ancient laws, such as those found in Deuteronomy, it becomes evident that they were crafted within a specific cultural and societal context, with considerations for protection, familial honor, and economic stability.

In antiquity, a woman's purity on her wedding night held immense value, both symbolically and economically. Families depended on this purity for income, and the maintenance of the family's reputation was paramount. Any question regarding a bride's virginity could tarnish the family name and impact the entire clan.

The law concerning a bride's virginity places the burden of proof on the parents in cases where accusations arise. This law serves as both protection and potential condemnation, as the family's reputation and financial stability hinge on the bride's purity. In some cases, families may stage innocence to protect their daughter, while in others, they may condemn her to safeguard their honor and marriage prospects for other

CHAPTER FOUR

family members.

The law regarding the rape of an unbetrothed virgin presents a complex scenario where marriage to the rapist is mandated. While this may seem unjust by modern standards, it was a form of protection for the victim, ensuring her future security and preventing her from being ostracized as unmarriageable. Additionally, the financial compensation provided by the rapist served as a form of restitution, reflecting the societal value placed on a woman's purity and potential marriageability.

The exchange of fifty shekels as compensation highlights the economic dimension of ancient laws, where financial transactions often played a significant role in legal matters. This amount, equivalent to a substantial wage, underscores the seriousness of the offense and the societal norms surrounding marriage and purity.

Through examining these ancient laws, we gain insight into the complexities of ancient society, where familial honor, economic stability, and societal norms intersected to shape legal and moral codes. While these laws may appear severe or outdated by modern standards, they reflect the intricate dynamics of ancient cultures and the efforts to maintain order, integrity, and protection within the community.

Contemplating ancient laws, such as those delineated in Deuteronomy, can evoke a range of emotions and reflections, particularly concerning the treatment of women in antiquity and its relevance to contemporary society.

Protection Amidst Vulnerability

Within the cultural context of ancient Israel, this law offered a form of protection for the victim. By mandating marriage to the perpetrator, the law ensured the victim's inclusion in society as a legitimate wife with rights, despite the traumatic circumstances of her union. Additionally, it provided an avenue for the victim to potentially become a mother and attain a sense of belonging within the community.

While aspects of ancient Jewish customs may be challenging to comprehend through a modern lens, they often represented a more compassionate and protective approach compared to neighboring cultures. The laws and customs of ancient Israel, rooted in Mosaic Law, aimed to safeguard the dignity and rights of individuals, including women, within the societal framework of that time.

Understanding the historical and cultural context of ancient laws offers valuable insights into the development of societal norms and customs, including those that have influenced Western Civilization. By examining these ancient principles, individuals, particularly women, can gain a deeper understanding of their inherent value and the enduring protection afforded to them by divine providence.

The exploration of ancient laws serves as a starting point for a broader examination of God's plan for humanity and the enduring relevance of foundational principles throughout history. By delving into the symbolism of Christ and his relationship with his bride, as depicted in Deuteronomy and beyond, individuals can glean profound insights into their own worth and purpose within the divine narrative.

As we continue our journey of exploration, let us seek to

uncover the timeless truths and enduring wisdom contained within ancient texts, recognizing their significance in shaping our understanding of identity, value, and destiny.

Chapter Four Summary

I recognize that this chapter contains a wealth of information, spanning topics such as sundry laws, slavery, blood rites, and customs regarding virginity. These study questions serve as a valuable tool to reinforce key details and concepts, aiding in the retention of knowledge. It may be beneficial to revisit the chapter to solidify your understanding before delving further into the subject matter.

Personally, I find that delving into the finer details is time well spent, as it deepens my comprehension and strengthens my connection with God. By examining Mosaic Law and the amendments found in Deuteronomy, we gain insight into the principles governing patriarchal responsibility and societal norms.

Our contemporary culture has evolved significantly, bringing both positive and negative changes. However, the innate desire for dominance remains prevalent among men. Yet, amidst these fluctuations, God's eternal wisdom and sovereignty endure. There is solace in knowing that nothing escapes His divine oversight, and His guidance remains steadfast throughout the ages..

Study questions for chapter four:

1-Which of the laws in Exodus and Deuteronomy are most engaging?

2- How are the ways the justice system today is based around and inspired by some of these laws?

3. Is a woman deprived today of not getting to celebrate her blood rites?

4. In what ways were the actions of men limited?

5. What is the highest purpose for a woman?

6. Have the study of any of these laws been enlightening, leading to deeper understanding?

7. How can one apply what they have learned?

Key points from chapter four

- Most of Mosaic Law is related to men and the dangers of domination.
- Mosaic Law is full of symbolism.
- The Israelites needed to identify with their sin.
- In Deuteronomy, God limits the actions of the man or the head of the household to protect his nation.
- Females, children, and slaves never spoke out of line or were allowed to voice their opinion in most cultures in antiquity.
- Under Mosaic Law, God even cared for stray animals.
- Females had certain blood rites.
- To be able to bear children was a commodity and a girl's family would achieve the highest price they could to improve status and wealth.

CHAPTER FOUR

Closing prayer for chapter four:

"Oh, Abba, Your Word is so rich and full of life and purpose. Thank You for revealing it to me. Thank You for Your Sovereignty and divine protection. Please teach me how to apply it and write it in my heart and mind. Please also continue investing in me Your truth. I understand You were calling man to account for his actions and to be responsible and that You wanted to purge Your chosen people from sin. For You are holy. What God is great like my God? There is none beside Thee. Amen."

Chapter Five

The Glory of the Law

It shall happen as God shall choose, for assuredly we lie not in our own power but the power of God. —Perpetua

In the culture I inhabit today, along with increased responsibility as a woman, comes the freedom to make choices. However, reflecting on the best decision I ever made brought me to a profound realization. When my stepson posed this question to me, I found myself momentarily speechless—a rare occurrence for someone who often speaks before fully listening. It was a humbling experience, reminding me of the wisdom in Proverbs 18:13: "He who answers before he hears, It is folly and shame to him."

As I contemplated my past decisions, I was initially overwhelmed by memories of mistakes and missteps. Yet, amidst the recollection of these errors, one pivotal moment stood out vividly. It took me back to 1979, a time when I encountered the Lamb of God at a crossroads. In that transformative moment, I chose to accept His grace and don the white robe of His righteousness. Looking back, I realized that this decision was undeniably the best one I ever made.

However, the process of arriving at this conclusion was both enlightening and humbling. It served as a poignant reminder that human intelligence alone cannot prevent sin or lead to salvation. Similarly, adherence to the law, without the necessary offerings and sacrifices for cleansing, could not save. These rituals were symbolic, foreshadowing the ultimate sacrifice that would bring true redemption.

In delving deeper into Mosaic Law, it becomes evident that understanding these statutes is crucial for grasping the essence of God's character. He desires to engage with every facet of His creation while respecting the free will bestowed upon humankind. At a time when people lived by their own moral compass, God intervened to establish a set of standards to safeguard the nation He had chosen through the faith of Abraham, nurturing them from a tribe into a nation. Despite being labeled as "stubborn and rebellious," this chosen nation was unique in acknowledging their Creator.

Exploring Marriage in Deuteronomy

While the initial verses of Deuteronomy 24 concerning divorce may appear straightforward, they hold profound symbolism. The groom mentioned in these verses represents Christ, who, akin to a devoted husband, would never forsake His bride. Christ's sacrificial act of dying for His bride serves as an eternal testament to His unwavering commitment. Furthermore, the guilt referenced in this chapter extends beyond individual sin, affecting the entire land and defiling the inheritance of the Lord. Symbolically, it signifies a rejection of Christ and His sacrifice, denying any rightful inheritance.

Deuteronomy 24:5 underscores the importance of marital satisfaction and honor within the context of Jewish customs. The provision for the husband to remain at home for a year after marriage reflects a commitment to prioritize the well-being and happiness of the wife. A harmonious marriage, marked by mutual fulfillment and adherence to God's design, is glorifying to Him. This period of marital bonding, supported financially by the husband or his family, lays a foundation for a healthy and prosperous union.

In Deuteronomy 25, the institution of levirate marriage emerges, mandating a man to wed his deceased brother's widow. This practice, rooted in Jewish custom, underscores familial responsibility and solidarity. Despite the seemingly trivial act of removing the shoe, it symbolizes a man's loss of dignity and unworthiness to stand on holy ground. By honoring this custom, individuals uphold the sanctity of their family name and respect for God's design.

In Deuteronomy verses 5-10, God's law addresses the delicate issue of ensuring the continuation of family lineage and securing an heir, especially in the context of levirate marriage. This provision offered protection to widows, preventing their marginalization and safeguarding their right to bear offspring to carry on the family name.

Communal Responsibility and Family Integrity

The law emphasized communal responsibility and family honor, deterring selfish motives among surviving brothers and ensuring that widows were not left destitute or ostracized. By upholding the dignity of widows and preserving the family's reputation, God's law fostered a sense of unity and integrity within the community.

This passage underscores God's concern for the vulnerable, particularly women, within society. By instituting laws that safeguarded their rights and ensured their welfare, God demonstrated His compassion and justice. Adherence to these laws became a testament to one's faith and trust in God's provision and care.

As Israel's population grew, adaptations of Mosaic Law in Deuteronomy aimed to address evolving social dynamics. While these changes benefited women by curbing the absolute authority of male heads of households, they also introduced complexities and challenges, altering power dynamics within families.

Protection of Sacred Symbols and Valuing Life

In the final law of Deuteronomy 25:11-12, God protects the sanctity of manhood by forbidding the striking of a man's genitals. This law underscores the inherent value of life and the importance of preserving sacred symbols, highlighting God's concern for the well-being and dignity of His creation.

In Deuteronomy, we witness God's intervention to hold dominant males accountable for their actions and to establish safeguards within the family unit. These laws reflect the importance of family integrity and address the consequences of male dominance in ancient society.

Drawing from stories in Genesis, such as the history of Judah and Tamar, Deuteronomy's laws offer protection to women in vulnerable situations, ensuring their rights and safety within the family structure. Reflecting on these narratives sheds light on the significance of God's intervention to prevent tragic outcomes.

Lot's actions in offering his daughters to the men of Sodom in Genesis 19 raise questions about moral responsibility and divine intervention. While some speculate on the motivations behind Lot's decision, the broader lesson underscores the importance of trusting in God's protection and guidance, even in moments of desperation and uncertainty.

The revelation of Sodom's impending destruction serves as a stark reminder of the unpredictability of life and the need for reliance on divine guidance. Despite the shock and disbelief faced by Lot and his family, their encounter with the angels highlights God's mercy and intervention in the face of impending judgment.

How would you respond today if some strangers knocked on your door and told you to flee, that the whole world around you was going to perish under the wrath of God?

You would have but one night to sort yourself out, you and your family.

What would you do if after you fled you saw everything

around you lit up in a blazing fire? Everything you owned. Gone.

What would you do if you thought you, your sister, and your father were the last people alive?

Compassion Amidst Human Frailty

When the time came for Lot and his family to abandon the city, his two future sons-in-law did not follow. This would relay to me that maybe they were not honorable men. They chose the world.

It may also be fair to surmise that just as their father lacked good judgment, so did the daughters. What would attract a God-fearing man to such a place, anyway? Perhaps riches, as this was a prosperous region. Further on in Genesis, after all the trauma, Lot and his daughters alone went to live in the mountains, and it is recorded that the girls believed they were the last people alive.

Lot's daughters' actions, though morally questionable, can be understood within the context of their fear and perceived duty to preserve humanity. Lacking understanding of the situation and living in a time before incest was explicitly forbidden, they resorted to drastic measures.

Their story parallels other biblical narratives where individuals, including Abraham, made decisions based on human reasoning rather than divine guidance. Just as Abraham's attempt to fulfill God's promise through Ishmael led to complications, Lot's daughters' actions resulted in long-term consequences for their descendants.

While acknowledging the mistakes of Lot's daughters and other biblical women like Eve, Sarah, and Rebekah, it is important to approach their stories with compassion. Like Adam,

Abraham, and Lot, they were not deemed evil for their failures but were products of their time and circumstances.

Their experiences serve as reminders of the complexities of human nature and the importance of relying on divine guidance rather than human reasoning alone. Despite their errors, they are not condemned but rather understood within the broader narrative of human fallibility and divine grace.

Deuteronomy's Social Message: Generational Responsibility

Deuteronomy conveys a social message emphasizing the responsibility of each generation to assist the next. This concept, reflected in modern governing systems, stems from Patriarchal Law established by God to protect and guide His chosen people, ensuring harmony and purity within the nation.

The Old Testament underscores the interconnectivity of individual actions and their impact on the community and the earth. Immorality and impurity among the Israelites led to decay and brought guilt upon the land, highlighting the need for adherence to God's laws for harmonious coexistence.

Instances such as idolatry, adultery, and rebellion in the Old Testament demonstrate the principle of collective guilt, where the actions of one individual affect the entire community or family. The stories of Achan, Dathan, Abiram, and Korah serve as stark reminders of the repercussions of individual transgressions on the wider community.

Conversely, strong faith can have a positive ripple effect, as exemplified by Noah's favor saving his family, Rahab's kindness leading to mercy for her household, and Obed-Edom's blessing for sheltering the ark. These narratives illustrate the power of righteousness to influence and protect loved ones.

Despite these examples, stories like the sexual abuse of Dinah and the disregard for women's value in incidents involving Lot's daughters and the Levite's concubine are difficult to reconcile. They highlight the historical devaluation of women and serve as poignant reminders of the need for societal transformation and gender equality.

Reevaluating the Story of Jephthah's Vow

The narrative of Jephthah's vow in Judges 11:29-40 has sparked controversy and varied interpretations. Jephthah, after making a vow to God, is compelled to sacrifice his only daughter upon his victory in battle However, the daughter's response to this fate deserves closer scrutiny.

Despite her grief the daughter displays unwavering obedience to her father's vow, prompting reflection on her character and upbringing. While Jephthah's faith has traditionally been lauded, his daughter's stoic acceptance of her fate raises questions about societal expectations and the treatment of women in ancient times.

A critical examination of Mosaic Law reveals God's disdain for human sacrifice, suggesting a deeper complexity to Jephthah's actions. Some argue that Jephthah's vow was a rash decision, while others speculate on alternative interpretations of the outcome.

While Hebrews 11 includes Jephthah in the Hall of Faith, his vow and its consequences remain subject to interpretation. Critics point out the incongruity of burnt sacrifices being limited to males, casting doubt on the traditional understanding of the story.

Ultimately, the story of Jephthah invites reflection on faith, obedience, and the complexities of human actions in the context of divine will. While the daughter's sacrifice is deeply troubling, the narrative prompts deeper exploration into the nuances of biblical interpretation and the moral implications of ancient customs.

Critics propose a reinterpretation of the story of Jephthah's vow, suggesting that his daughter's fate was not literal human sacrifice but rather the loss of her virginity and the inability to bear children. Here are key points supporting this perspective:

1. Two-Month Mourning Period: The daughter's request for a two-month mourning period is interpreted as mourning her virginity, as she would never be able to marry and fulfill her role as a mother. This highlights the significance of offspring in ancient society and underscores the tragedy of her sacrifice.
2. Only Child: The text specifies that Jephthah's daughter was his only child, emphasizing the extinction of his family line. In antiquity, progeny were paramount, adding depth to the tragedy of her fate.
3. Treatment of Sacrifice: The sacrifice is portrayed as unfortunate not because of concern over death but because of the loss of the daughter's potential as a mother. Jephthah's distress stems from her perpetual virginity, not her death.

The verse in Judges 11:39, stating that Jephthah did to her according to his vow and she remained celibate, supports this interpretation. If her fate were literal sacrifice, it would be sacrilegious and contrary to God's principles, as human sacrifice was never sanctioned except for the sacrifice of Christ, the final lamb.

In essence, the sacrifice of Jephthah's daughter symbolizes the loss of her future as a mother and the extinction of Jephthah's family line, rather than her literal death as an offering to God.

Reflections on Mosaic Law and Women in the Old Testament

Through an examination of Mosaic Law and controversial texts concerning women in the Old Testament, we find insights into God's perspective and intent. This exploration dispels suspicions of male favoritism by God and reveals the inherent equality of men and women, each endowed with distinct characteristics to complement one another.

The narrative underscores Satan's relentless targeting of women since the fall of Adam and Eve, driven by his desire to thwart the propagation of the Savior's seed. Evidence of men's sins infiltrating their family lines is scattered throughout the Old Testament, emphasizing the covenantal blessing bestowed upon Abraham's seed through faith.

Additionally, the role of women in traditional synagogue and temple services is examined, highlighting the influence of rabbinic tradition on gender dynamics. However, the promise of equality in worship is envisioned through the imagery of the New Jerusalem, where all will worship together without distinction.

While the Old Testament may appear to favor men, a closer examination reveals greater concern for the conduct of men than women. God's laws, intended to protect and benefit humanity, emphasized individual accountability and collective responsibility, contrasting with the lack of accountability in contemporary society.

In sharing these insights, the aim is to empower women with an understanding of God's love, protection, and desire for their thriving in the world. Moving forward, further exploration will illuminate the treatment of women in the New Testament, particularly through the life and example of Jesus.

Chapter Five Summary

Reading the Old Testament, it is understandable that women feel that men receive preferential treatment. By unpacking the culture in antiquity and putting parts of Mosaic Law under the lens, we find far more concerns about the conduct of men than of women. Until a different law was given, the old laws of God were binding. Their purpose has always been to protect, benefit, and save humanity. And just as God spoke through the prophet Moses in Deuteronomy, those who kept his law were blessed; those who did not keep it were broken. Today people try to improve the laws God originally ordained while rejecting God.

The Old Testament stresses that an individual should not behave as if what he does has no bearing or effect on others. It also testifies that the guilt of one law meant guilt of the entire law. We can clearly understand that the guilt of one person not only bled over into the tribe, but it brought guilt to the land. In society today, people have no such accountability. This chapter also gives us a glimpse at God's intentions for his people foreshadowing the coming church.

CHAPTER FIVE

Study questions for chapter five:

1. How did the state of Israel differ from the rest of the known world?

2. What was the purpose of the Mosaic Law?

3. How does this law bring a social message to the nation of Israel?

4. Why did the guilt of one bring guilt upon the entire tribe?

5. From what has been taught so far, what has had the biggest effect on
    you?

6. How did God's intervention with the laws and the protection of women upset Israel for all of history?

7. What is the most important thing to remember about the message in
    Deuteronomy?

Key points from chapter five:

- Only Israel acknowledged their Creator.
- The laws in Deuteronomy reveal the heart of God towards the chosen nation he was birthing.
- The laws in Deuteronomy were adapted from the earlier laws in Exodus as the nation grew.
- God was making the paterfamilias responsible.

- Throughout the course of history, some great women who were trying to help their husbands failed miserably.
- Deuteronomy brings a social message to the Israelites.
- God wanted to purge the nation to keep his people pure.
- God set up laws to keep his people living in harmony with the earth he created for them.
- When the nation was in sin, they also brought guilt on the land.
- The guilt of one meant guilt of the whole tribe.
- Satan hates women most as they bear offspring.
- Abraham received blessing not by works, but by faith.
- Until a new law was given, the old laws of God were binding.
- Those who kept God's laws were blessed; those who did not were broken.

Closing prayer for chapter five:

"Abba, Your wisdom and long-suffering are remarkable. Your master plan is exceptional. Your love for Your people is undeniable. I am not worthy that You should take note of me and bring me into the knowledge of Your ways and purposes. I am but dust. For who among men can give You counsel? You call the stars by name and tell the waves where they can go no further. Yet You pay me great attention and give me much protection. You never sleep, Abba. Thank You. Thank You for unveiling the symbolism of the Mosaic Law. Thank You for showing me that it all points to the coming of the one final law under Christ Jesus. And thank You for fulfilling the law. Please keep drawing close to me and teaching me Your ways. Help Your daughters to see their equality in Your eyes. Help women to understand that You will make everything beautiful in time. Amen."

Chapter Six

Women and the Household of God

> When I get to heaven, the first face that shall ever gladden my sight will be that of my Savior. —Fanny Crosby

Words are powerful things. In this book, I have tried to master them carefully and prayerfully. As I delve into the depths of God's Law, my heart swells with an indescribable passion. Each revelation, each insight, is a glimpse into the very heart of God Himself. With each word penned, I am compelled to graciously share the treasures I uncover, for the Word of God is not mere ink on paper—it is life-giving, a balm for the weary soul.

My fervor is not merely for understanding equality or unraveling ancient customs; these are but facets of a greater truth. At the core of my being lies a vibrant connection to the source of all life: Jesus Christ. He is the hub of the wheel, the anchor of my existence. Without Him, I am adrift, unable to comprehend, let alone embrace, the profound wisdom contained within God's Law.

Through my words, I seek to uplift and edify, to strengthen and support, those who journey alongside me. For in Christ, we find not only knowledge but transformation. As we immerse ourselves in His truth, we are renewed, empowered to walk in His ways and reflect His glory to the world.

Transitioning to the New Testament: A Journey of Revelation

As we transition from exploring the laws of the Patriarchs and delving into the intricacies of Mosaic Law, we stand on the threshold of a profound revelation. The customs and traditions that have favored the Patriarchal system are about to be challenged by the unveiling of one final law—the Law of Christ.

In preparation for this paradigm shift, it's crucial to grasp the significance of this law and its implications for women. While it may stir controversy in some quarters, my intention is not to incite debate but to spread the liberating truth that awaits within.

Before delving into the Law of Christ, let us first recognize the profound nature of His existence. In the Gospel of John, we are confronted with the truth that Jesus Christ is not only a historical figure but the embodiment of the Word of God. In the opening verses of John 1:1-3, we are told, "In the beginning was the Word, and the Word was with God, and the Word was God."

Pause for a moment to contemplate this profound revelation. Jesus Christ is not merely a man; He is the Word incarnate—the divine expression of God Himself. He descended from the spiritual realm, assuming human form to dwell among us. As the Word, He embodies both the spiritual and physical realms, making Himself known through His spoken and written word.

Let us marvel at the mystery of His incarnation and embrace the truth that He is the ultimate revelation of God's love and redemption for humanity. As we embark on this journey through the New Testament, may our hearts be open to the transformative power of the Word made flesh, Jesus Christ.

So the Word came in the flesh to save and minister to his created beings!

Indeed, as the Word made flesh, Jesus not only walked among us but also left a part of Himself with us—in spirit and in the written truth of Scripture—to guide, comfort, and enlighten us on our journey of faith. And at the same time he was with God... And still is! Can you get your head around it?

Truly, everything we perceive and beyond was brought into existence by this Word. It is a continuous flow of truth in flesh and spirit, constantly creating, breathing, and speaking. The Word is awesome, magnificent, majestic, and powerful—a Sovereign being beyond compare.

Through this Word, Christ, a new law was given, passed down through the Apostles and enacted through the perfect sacrifice of Christ's death. This law was given to all nations. It is the Law of Liberty.

Let us now begin to unpack the impacting passages in the New Testament, turning our attention first to Acts.

CHAPTER SIX

Jesus Freed Us From All Things

Acts 13:39, "And through him, everyone who believes is freed from all things, from which one could not be freed through the Law of Moses."

This is the perfect verse to link the Old and New Testaments. Just what does this liberty look like?

Indeed, I am no longer bound by the Patriarchal Law or the Mosaic Law! This liberation extends both physically and spiritually—I am freed from the duties imposed by the law, and spiritually, I am no longer tethered to the realm of death or the body of the first Adam.

Christ serves as the fulfillment and the payment for the law, simultaneously covering and surpassing its requirements. The Law is now completed, finished, and superseded by grace. Any attempt to return to the age of Mosaic Law is a sin, a rejection of the magnificent work accomplished by Jesus.

With Christ's death came the end of the Age of Mosaic Law and the beginning of the Age of Grace. This new law, binding until Christ's return, is upheld by the Holy Spirit dwelling within me—a deposit guaranteeing the fulfillment of God's promises. Until then, I must diligently adhere to this new law, embracing its spiritual essence while also following its physical and moral precepts.

Jesus and Women

Jesus' relationship with women during his ministry was revolutionary and controversial, shaking the foundations of societal norms and cultural customs. While many are familiar with his teachings, miracles, and compassionate acts, the profound impact of his interactions with women is often overlooked.

Jesus challenged societal conventions by dining with tax collectors, who were considered traitors, and associating with women labeled as sinners. In a culture where respectable women and men rarely socialized together, Jesus' actions were radical. Women were typically marginalized, unable to give testimony in court or address men outside their immediate family.

By engaging with women as equals and showing them compassion and respect, Jesus demonstrated a profound shift in attitudes towards women. His actions challenged entrenched prejudices and emphasized the equal worth and dignity of all individuals, regardless of gender.

Examples of Equality Under Christ

The following biblical examples vividly illustrate how Jesus defied societal norms and cultural conventions regarding the treatment of women. Despite the prevailing attitudes of his time, Jesus consistently demonstrated a radical inclusivity and equality in his interactions with women, challenging the restrictive rules enforced by religious leaders.

Consider these instances:

- **Mark 5:25-34**: Jesus addresses a woman suffering from a 12-year hemorrhage, disregarding the social taboo against unrelated men speaking to women. He not only speaks to her but also commends her faith, affirming her worth and dignity.
- **Matthew 15:22-28**: Jesus engages in conversation with a Canaanite woman, breaking cultural barriers and recogniz-

ing her faith despite societal prejudices.
- **John 4:7-40**: Jesus converses with a Samaritan woman, treating her as an equal and empowering her to become an evangelist, challenging gender and cultural boundaries.
- **Luke 10:38-42**: Jesus encourages Mary to prioritize spiritual understanding over traditional gender roles, affirming the value of women's contributions in the Kingdom of God.
- **Luke 13:10-17**: Jesus heals a woman on the Sabbath, affirming her dignity and worth as a "daughter of Abraham" and challenging legalistic interpretations of the Sabbath law.
- **Matthew 27:55-56, John 19:25-27**: Women are prominently featured at Jesus' crucifixion, demonstrating their courage and commitment, in contrast to the absence of most male disciples.
- **Matthew 28:1-10**: Women are the first witnesses to Jesus' resurrection and are entrusted with proclaiming the good news to the male disciples, underscoring their essential role in the spread of the gospel.

These examples reveal Jesus' revolutionary approach to gender equality and his affirmation of women's value and agency in the Kingdom of God. His actions challenged entrenched social norms and empowered women to fulfill significant roles in his ministry and the spread of the gospel.

We will delve into the passages that often spark heated debates and divisions, particularly between spouses and believers. These passages, while seemingly contradictory at times, share a common thread: the metaphor of the household. By considering this overarching theme, we can gain a deeper understanding of God's intentions and reconcile apparent contradictions.

The Household as a Metaphor

Throughout the New Testament, the household serves as a recurring metaphor, reflecting the cultural significance of familial relationships. By examining how various biblical texts employ this metaphor, we can discern the underlying principles guiding interpersonal dynamics within the church and society.

Each local church faced unique challenges and contexts, influencing the messages conveyed in the Pauline epistles and other New Testament writings. By considering the historical and cultural backdrop of these communities, we can better grasp the intended meanings behind the instructions regarding gender roles and relationships.

One thing I want to emphasize: When approaching God's Word and trying to understand it, we must not read our culture into it. Ever.

Ultimately, our goal is to harmonize the diverse perspectives presented in the New Testament regarding women's roles. By placing these pieces together and discerning the underlying principles, we can affirm the consistency and integrity of God's Word, despite differing interpretations and cultural contexts.

In order to succeed, we must stop viewing the culture and lifestyle of that past as if it were like that of today. Stop reading our culture into the Bible. This is extremely difficult!

As we consider the complexities and trials within the contemporary church body, it's essential to recognize the influence of societal temptations and deceptions. Just as the people in antiquity were shaped by their surroundings, so too are modern-day believers affected by the culture around them.

CHAPTER SIX

Reflecting on the Church as a Body

One prevalent challenge facing the church today is the temptation to prioritize material wealth and worldly success. In many institutions and operations, money has become the central driving force, potentially overshadowing the guidance of the Holy Spirit. This shift can lead to the idolization of pastors and other leaders, blurring the line between spiritual authority and celebrity status.

The infiltration of cultural practices into the church is not a new phenomenon. Throughout history, the church has grappled with the influence of societal norms and values. Today, as in antiquity, believers must navigate the tension between remaining faithful to biblical principles and adapting to the cultural context in which they live.

Examining the basic structure of Jewish life during the time of Christ provides insight into the concept of the household. While the modern definition of "family" may vary, the ancient understanding of the household encompassed not only immediate family members but also extended relatives, servants, possessions, and even land. Understanding these dynamics helps us grasp the interconnectedness of individuals within the broader social framework.

The Greco-Roman Household: A Complex Unit

During the time of Christ and the writings of the New Testament, the Greco-Roman household stood as a formidable institution. It was not merely a dwelling but also a bustling business enterprise, encompassing all members of the family, servants, slaves, workers, tenants, livestock, and material possessions.

At the helm of the household was the paterfamilias, the patriarch who wielded absolute authority and ownership over all within his domain. He was typically the oldest male in the household and oversaw its growth, stability, and worship practices.

In modern Western civilization, the concept of family may revolve around biological relations, including extended relatives such as cousins, uncles, aunts, and grandparents. However, in the Greco-Roman world, family identity was deeply intertwined with the patrilineal lineage, focusing primarily on the male patriarchs and their descendants.

Marriage in Greco-Roman society was not based solely on romantic love but rather served as a binding legal contract. Its primary purposes were to elevate the status of each family, produce legitimate offspring, and ensure the transfer of property to future generations. Love, as we understand it today, may not have been a central consideration in these unions.

The Greek philosopher Demosthenes said it best around the fourth century BC, "We have courtesans for our pleasure, prostitutes for daily physical use, wives to bring up legitimate children and to be faithful stewards in household matters."

Status of Women in Roman and Greek Societies

In ancient times, particularly within monarchies, courtesans played a significant role as companions to rulers, providing intimate affairs and entertainment within the court. These women, often wealthy and talented, served as entertainers and offered amorous attention to the monarchs. Over time, some royal women also maintained male courtesans.

By the eighteenth century, courtesans had evolved into individuals who offered seduction and companionship to wealthy clients in exchange for material possessions such as money, jewelry, and property.

Historically, Roman women enjoyed higher status and more independence compared to their Greek counterparts. Roman wives could even become the head of the household after the death of their husbands. However, Greek philosophy often portrayed women as over-emotional and intellectually inferior, advocating for their subordination to men. Greek society placed strict restrictions on women's public appearances and social interactions, emphasizing their roles within the household and family sphere.

Influence of Greek Thought on Jewish Teaching

During the Second Temple Era, Jewish Rabbis began incorporating Greek philosophical ideas into their teachings, leading to the devaluation of women within Jewish society. Concepts such as women's inferiority to men and Eve as a prototype for womankind being connected with sin and deception became prevalent.

It's crucial for every woman to be aware of these historical truths, as they shed light on the origins of gender inequalities and challenge the notion of divine ordinance in their subjugation. By embracing these truths, women can gain a deeper understanding of their societal roles and advocate for their rights and equality.

In ancient Rome and Greece, women transitioned from being under the authority of their fathers to their husbands upon marriage. Even after marriage, a woman's primary allegiance often remained with her father's family. Divorce would result in the return of the dowry to the woman's father's house, highlighting the financial and familial dynamics at play in marriage contracts.

Historical records indicate that emotional bonds between spouses and parents and children were often secondary in importance. Factors such as high mortality rates, pagan rituals, and societal perceptions of children as property contributed to the complexities of familial relationships in ancient societies, challenging modern notions of familial bonds and love.

Historical Perspectives on Familial Relationships

In ancient societies, such as Greco-Roman culture, familial dynamics were vastly different from modern notions. Contrary to present-day norms, the most intimate relationships were often between siblings, rather than between parents and children. Emotional bonds, particularly romanticism, were generally not prominent until the Renaissance period, reshaping societal perceptions of relationships.

Sibling relationships held significant importance, with the phrase "closer than a brother" highlighting the strength of these connections. Throughout history and literature, conflicts and alliances among siblings are recurrent themes, emphasizing the deep-seated familial ties within ancient societies.

Drawing parallels between ancient households and the modern church, questions arise regarding the role of authority. While some may view the pastor as the paterfamilias of the church, it is essential to recognize that this role should be reserved for God alone. However, the misconception persists, leading to potential abuses of power within congregations.

CHAPTER SIX

Maintaining Historical Context in Biblical Interpretation

Understanding the historical context of familial relationships is crucial when interpreting biblical passages. By acknowledging the cultural differences and societal norms of ancient times, readers can gain deeper insights into the intended messages of scripture and avoid imposing modern interpretations onto ancient texts.

The family business and land have been the standard in most civilizations since time began. By the time Christ was born, women were getting more liberties. This was because there was turmoil and indecision in the Empire and mystical goddesses were being worshiped in place of the dying view of the Roman gods. That practice was spreading quickly from the East, specifically amongst women, slaves, and anyone with lower status. But amongst the wealthy, they held the conservative view on traditional Roman religion, and anyone going against this view was perceived as a threat to the Empire.

Status and Influence in the Greco-Roman World

In the Greco-Roman period, status was not primarily determined by political power or wealth, but by a concept known as "charis." Charis referred to the number of clients one could obtain, establishing a patron-client relationship. The patron provided significant favors to clients, who in turn owed loyalty and support. Thus, expanding one's network of clients elevated one's status, creating a hierarchical pyramid of influence.

Greek philosophical teachings permeated Greco-Roman culture, influencing societal norms and perceptions. These teachings, combined with mystic beliefs in goddesses, shaped the worldview of the people. However, they also introduced biases and prejudices, such as the prayer of thanksgiving uttered by Jewish men, expressing gratitude for not being born as women, Gentiles, or slaves.

When reading the New Testament, it's crucial to understand the cultural context and the layers of translation that believers had to navigate. They had to interpret the teachings of Christ within the framework of Ancient Near Eastern culture, Greco-Roman society, and Jewish Mosaic Law, while also embracing the transformative message of the new law in Christ. This multi-layered perspective sheds light on the challenges faced by early Christians in contextualizing their faith within diverse cultural landscapes.

Jesus' Higher Moral Code

In Matthew 5, Jesus delivers the Sermon on the Mount, ushering in the new law that stands until his return. He elevates the moral standards, revealing that hatred equates to murder and lustful looks to adultery. Notably, while women were historically more restricted in committing adultery, Jesus equalizes the boundary for both men and women, holding them to the same standard...and the safe fate.

Jesus disrupts societal norms by removing men's liberty and liberating women, making the law more binding. He addresses the root of adultery, starting with the eye and hand, recognizing the heart's weakness. Regarding divorce, traditionally permitted by men, Jesus restricts it, allowing only in cases of infidelity. He emphasizes the husband's responsibility, attributing guilt if divorce occurs and condemning remarriage as adultery, protecting women from unjust divorces and ensuring their financial security. Men were changing wives like they changed their underwear simply for sake of pleasure.

By challenging the validity of all divorces before God and defending unwillingly divorced women, Jesus upholds integrity and advocates for women's rights beyond societal norms. His teachings emphasize justice, equality, and compassion, reflecting God's heart for all individuals, particularly those vulnerable to societal injustices.

In the Sermon on the Mount, Jesus confronts the prevalent abuse of marriage and divorce, primarily by men who would dismiss their wives for trivial reasons or with mere verbal declarations. This abuse reflected a societal degradation of marriage, akin to the Islamic practice of instantaneous divorce pronouncements.

Jesus's prohibition of divorce, even for men, is not a literal decree but a powerful statement intended to address the pervasive issue of marital exploitation and to protect women from harm. By making such an extreme statement, Jesus highlights the seriousness of marriage and challenges the prevailing cultural attitudes towards it.

His overarching message throughout the sermon is one of integrity, urging individuals to overcome selfish desires and elevate their moral standards. Rather than condemning divorced individuals, Jesus's words emphasize personal accountability and a call to uphold the sanctity of marriage.

This interpretation offers a nuanced understanding of Jesus's teachings on divorce, encouraging deeper reflection and accountability among believers, and fostering a compassionate approach towards those affected by divorce.

A Call for Contextual Understanding

Matthew 5:32 has often been wielded as a condemnation of divorced individuals who remarry, suggesting that they commit adultery. However, a closer examination of its context reveals a deeper meaning that transcends simplistic interpretations.

Rather than imposing modern cultural norms onto this verse, it is essential to understand it within the cultural context of Jesus's time. Jesus's words were not meant to restrict divorced women from remarrying but to address the prevalent issue of divorce and remarriage in his society.

Jesus did not initiate a civil rights movement or advocate for social upheaval. Instead, he focused on serving others and challenging the prevailing attitudes of status and righteousness. His teachings turned societal norms upside down, emphasizing humility, compassion, and integrity over status-seeking and self-righteousness.

By reframing our understanding of Matthew 5:32 within its cultural context, we can glean a more nuanced interpretation that emphasizes compassion and understanding rather than judgment and condemnation.

We can better understand the radical changes laid out in this list:

Status under Society:
1-Paterfamilias
2-Wife
3-Children
4-Servants
5-Slaves

Status under Jesus:
1-Slaves

2-Servants
3-Children
4-Wife
5-Paterfamilias

In the societal hierarchy of Jesus' time, the paterfamilias held the highest status, wielding authority over all within his household. However, Jesus challenged this norm by exalting the role of the servant, elevating the slave to the highest status within his spiritual household.

Jesus' teachings emphasized a radical reversal of societal values, where the first would become last and the last would become first, echoing his own title as the First and the Last. In his life, Jesus embodied both servant and master, exemplifying humility and authority in equal measure.

When Jesus addressed the people, his words stunned them, challenging them to strive for a level of righteousness that seemed unattainable. Yet, those who grasped his wisdom understood the eternal significance of his teachings and their profound need for him.

Continuing his revolutionary message, Jesus delivered an address in Matthew 6 and 7 that laid down a new law, reshaping the course of history with its profound insights and challenges.

Embracing the New Kingdom Order

The selection of the twelve disciples by Jesus carried profound symbolic significance, signaling the emergence of a new Israel with each disciple representing a head of one of the tribes. Through this choice, Jesus foreshadowed a future where his followers would stand in judgment over the tribes, united as one family under his divine leadership.

Jesus challenged societal norms by demanding that allegiance to the spiritual Kingdom of God supersede biological family ties. By using the household as a metaphor, Jesus enabled his audience to grasp the essence of a deep relationship with God and one another, anticipating the coming realities of their future relationship with God in the age of shalom.

Reflecting on the life of Christ fills me with awe and joy, witnessing the profound impact he had on society. Jesus elevated the lowly and disrespected, diminishing the role of the paterfamilias and uplifting those society had marginalized.

His choice of disciples—fishermen, tax collectors, women, and slaves—testifies to his radical inclusivity and compassion. At the foot of the cross, I find solace, knowing that my sins are forgiven and my wounds will be transformed into beautiful scars as I strive to emulate the status code of Christ, embracing humility, servanthood, and love.

Chapter Six Summary

Our journey into the New Testament unveils the final law of God—the Law of Liberty. Through radical observations into the life of Christ, we witness his transformative treatment of women, reshaping societal norms and challenging the dominance of the paterfamilias.

A pivotal moment occured as Jesus conversed with the Samaritan woman at the well, revealing his identity and sparking a ripple effect of evangelism and testimony. With minimal words, Jesus conveyed profound truths, urging his disciples to seek status in his kingdom where brotherly bonds reign supreme.

From the mountaintop, Jesus delivered earth-shaking revelations, introducing the Law of Liberty. He unveiled the gravity of adultery, equating lust with guilt, and condemning hatred as equivalent to murder. These teachings challenged societal boundaries, yet many, like the Pharisees and Sadducees, resisted embracing them.

In elevating the status of women and exhorting integrity, Jesus set a new standard for humanity—one rooted in love, humility, and accountability before God. As we navigate the Law of Liberty, we recognize our collective guilt and the transformative power of Christ's teachings.

Study questions for chapter six:

1. What does it mean that Jesus was the Word in the flesh?

2. What are some of the things Jesus did away with that helped advance women?

3. Has the church today got a good hold of the context of Jesus' message on divorce and integrity?

4. What was Jesus trying to signify on the Sermon on the Mount?

5. Does the body of Christ today portray well the first-last scenario?

6. How are people affected today by Jesus using household metaphors?

7. How can one apply what they have learned from this chapter?

Key points from chapter six:

- Jesus is the fulfillment of the Mosaic Law, which I never need to adhere to again.
- Jesus was quite virtually the Word in the flesh.
- The new law is binding until Christ returns.
- Jesus' entire ministry was controversial and revolutionary.
- Jesus was called a wine-bibber and friend of sinners.
- Jesus treated men and women equally.
- I must stop reading my culture into the Bible.
- The closest bonds in antiquity were between siblings.
- In the mainstream, worship of the Roman Gods was dying and being replaced with the worship of goddesses.
- Status was the most important thing in the Greco-Roman period.
- Jesus speaks of a higher code to live by on the Sermon on the Mount.
- Jesus addressed men who were disposing of their wives cheaply.
- Jesus taught people to have integrity.

CHAPTER SIX

Closing prayer for chapter six:

"Abba, Your life in the flesh was incredible. It is so hard to understand that You were the Word and that You sat in the heavenly places. That You came down as the Word wrapped in the form of a baby. You revolutionized modern thought and elevated the status of women above the paterfamilias. You made the slave worthy. And You spoke to me in a way that I could understand. You know me so intimately. Thank You. Thank You for making everything new. Forgive me when I put myself and my flesh above You and take for granted all that You have done when I moan and forget I am Your beloved, Your heir. Amen."

Chapter Seven

The Household and the Bride

G*uided by God, she pressed on until after a time she reached what she had longed for, the holiest places of the birth, passion, and resurrection of the Lord.* —Egeria

Encountering Jesus in 1979 was a turning point that completely transformed my life. Before that moment, I lacked confidence, struggled to find my voice, and felt a void of love in my life. But as soon as Jesus became real to me, everything changed.

Suddenly, I found a newfound confidence within myself. Words flowed more freely, and I discovered the depth of love that had been missing. It's incredible how these seemingly small changes had such a profound impact on me, breaking down the barriers that once held me back.

Decades later, as I sit here, I'm reminded of the incredible transformation that occurred in my life. It's a powerful testament to the ongoing growth and renewal that comes from surrendering to Christ. The birth, life, death, and resurrection of Jesus were so profound. Particularly for women.

What a journey it has been.

Exploring Ancient Household Layouts: Insights into Daily Life

As I delved deeper into my research, I stumbled upon architectural layouts of various households, each offering a glimpse into daily life during ancient times. One such layout depicted the average household found within a village setting.

In most villages, the layout revolved around a central spring or well, serving as a focal point for the community. The houses themselves were typically constructed using wattle-and-daub or baked clay and straw, reflecting the available resources and building techniques of the time.

Studying the accompanying graphic provided valuable insight into the structure and organization of these households. It became evident that daily life unfolded within the confines of the home, encompassing a wide range of activities such as work, childcare, education, and leisure.

Interestingly, despite the cultural ideal of a large, patriarchal family, the actual size of an average household was likely smaller, often comprising fewer than eight individuals. This discrepancy can be attributed to the high mortality rate prevalent during that era. Men, on average, lived to around 40 years old, while women had a life expectancy of approximately 36 years.

Within these households, it was customary for three generations to coexist under one roof: parents, unmarried children, married sons and their wives, and grandchildren. Additionally, extended families often lived in close proximity to one another, either within the same dwelling or neighboring houses, fostering a strong sense of community and interconnectedness.

Artist's reconstruction of a four-room house:

Model courtesy of Nick Laarakkers

1: central activity area

2: stable area

3: storage room

4: sleeping quarters

5: clay roof

1-The inside of the living quarters was generally white plaster. The entrance would lead into here. Most household tasks took place in this area, such as food preparation and eating, teaching, and the like. If the house was large, a courtyard could be in the center with rooms surrounding it and maybe a skylight. This room was probably divided by pillars.

2-On the other side of the pillars would be cobblestone, generally to the side. This space was used for food storage and as a stable.

3-To the rear was another room, typically long and wide, used for long-term storage.

4-The sleeping area was on the second floor. It may also have been used for entertaining. Stairs or wooden ladders were used to reach this floor. The walls were constructed with roughly hewn blocks of stone.

5-The roof was made from wooden beams layered with branches and smooth clay. For additional living space, a wooden ladder or stairs could have gone up to the roof from outside.

Daily Life in Ancient Villages: Women's Activities and Food Culture

Due to a mild climate, many daily activities in ancient villages likely took place outdoors. Women commonly tended to plots of land or gardens on the outskirts of the village, primarily used for growing food. However, decorative gardens were a luxury reserved for the wealthy due to the constraints of time and money.

Regular trips to the market were essential for women to purchase necessities, although wealthier women often delegated this task to their slaves. The staple food in Jewish households was bread, typically made from barley and ground between stones by women. Wealthier families could afford wheat bread.

Women were responsible for grinding and kneading the dough for baking, which was done on an open fire. Jewish meals often included unleavened bread, which was pliable and versatile. Locusts, a common addition to flour, were debated to be either the insect or the carob fruit, known for its nutritional value.

Milk from sheep and goats was used for drinking, butter, and cheese-making, while honey served as a primary sweetener along with grape or date juice. Dinner typically consisted of vegetables, beans, lentils, cucumbers, onions, and occasionally fish or poultry, depending on the household's wealth and proximity to the coast.

In ancient villages, meat was a luxury reserved for special occasions, while staples like figs, dates, grapes, and dried fruits were common in everyday meals. Olives were primarily used for oil, and a variety of spices, including mustard, capers, cumin, saffron, and mint, were used for seasoning. Wine, typically diluted with water 3-1, was a common beverage, although strong wine was considered socially unacceptable except for the wealthy. Consequently, strong wine is the type of wine we drink today.

Despite the challenges of daily life, the Jewish community enjoyed entertaining guests and valued communal living for practical and social reasons. Living in such a communal setting, with reliance on one another for various needs, likely provided a sense of satisfaction and fulfillment, especially when coupled with a life centered on the promises of God.

Drawing from personal experience living in a small village in the Sierra Nevada Mountains of Spain, I can attest to the satisfaction derived from such a lifestyle. The Mediterranean climate and abundance of fruits and nuts year-round provided ample opportunities for harvesting and enjoying nature's bounty. In such close-knit communities, outdoor living was common, and the safety and peacefulness of village life allowed children to roam freely, even late into the night.

Common Villas in Antiquity

A couple of years back, I visited Pompeii. I was in awe. I could just absorb what a quality of life the people had made for themselves. Trying to picture it in all its earthly grandeur, I imagined marble facades over the entire city, with mosaics, and frescoes. There was a well-developed sewer system and central heating, too. The rich had grand courtyards with fountains and pools. Roses abounded and were used for decoration, adorning the hair, perfume, and cuisine.

The model house below would represent the ones I viewed in Pompeii. It portrays a good picture of what houses of the wealthy looked like in Israel under Roman occupation as well. As one might expect, the houses of the rich were constructed of quality materials and more spacious. A rich woman would have a fireplace and a tile floor and a servant to sweep it, while the average Jewish woman would sweep a clay floor in front of a brazier.

CHAPTER SEVEN

"A Pompeian Interior" by Luig Bazzani (1882)

The Evolution of Rural Villas: From Pleasure Domes to Agricultural Centers

During the era leading up to the New Testament, the wealthiest Romans began constructing rural villas on the outskirts of villages. These villas served as luxurious retreats, akin to modern-day summer homes, where the elite could escape the hustle and bustle of city life.

While the owners indulged in leisure and pleasure at these villas, the less fortunate, including the very poor and slaves, often resided there as well, likely working the land or engaging in mining activities. Some of these villas were expansive enough to resemble small towns, accommodating hundreds of individuals within the household.

The more prestigious villas were primarily used for agricultural purposes, reflecting the importance of land ownership and cultivation in Roman society. In cases where the villa owners preferred to reside primarily in their central village house, they would appoint a landlord to oversee the management of the villa on a permanent basis.

Understanding the dynamics of rural villas and their inhabitants provides valuable context for interpreting Jesus' teachings and parables, shedding light on the socioeconomic realities of the time and how they intersected with everyday life.

CHAPTER SEVEN

A Roman Villa in antiquity containing a large household

Within the villa, there would be many different businesses like blacksmiths, bakers, rug weavers, fabric and dye makers, stable keepers, gardeners. There were field workers who lived in small huts with their families around the villa. Some were free workers renting the land they worked, others slaves. The rent would be paid with a share of the crops. There were orchards, herb gardens, flower gardens, and vineyards along with lots of animals. Villas this size would be self-sufficient. Some of these households were so strong that after the fall of the Roman Empire, they went on to become small established villages.

I dream about what a wonderful existence this could have

been, so much closer to nature than our world today.

In the parable where Jesus speaks of the master who leaves his servant in charge while he goes away on business, this is the type of villa that Jesus was most likely referring to.

Outside of the city, there was no law enforcement and nearly every large villa contained its own prison for disciplining the slave, for example, as they were outside the Roman penal system. The passage in Matthew comes to mind in chapters 8:10-12 "When Jesus heard him, he was amazed and said to those who followed him, 'Truly I tell you, in no one in Israel have I found such faith. I tell you, many will come from east and west and will eat with Abraham and Isaac and Jacob in the kingdom of heaven, while the heirs of the kingdom will be thrown into the outer darkness, where there will be weeping and gnashing of teeth.'"

These villa prisons were windowless and dark where people could actually be heard weeping and gnashing their teeth.

There was one last type of household, the insulae. These urban dwellings were popularizing before the time of Christ, and they were like apartments today. They were the living quarters of small shopkeepers, above the storefronts. As concrete was improving in its make-up, more stories or levels were being developed.

In the diagram, the apartment block was surrounding a couple of wells with a toilet on each floor. The number "1" marking on the first floor indicates the shops while on the second floor the "2" marking would be apartments with a single balcony at the front. The difference between the insulae and the previous dwellings was that it did not comprise a household; rather, it was formed of many different households.

CHAPTER SEVEN

Understanding Jesus' Ministry Through the Lens of Household Metaphors

Now that we have delved into the concept of households in ancient Israel, we can gain deeper insights into the ministry of Jesus. As the embodiment of the Law and the Prophets, Jesus introduced a new law, and his teachings often utilized household metaphors to convey profound truths. Let's explore some of these metaphors, beginning with the relationship between husbands and wives, as presented in Matthew 19:3-12.

Jesus, embodying the new law while fulfilling the old, unveils profound truths about marriage in Matthew 19:3-12. He pierces the hearts of those who seek to justify their actions, declaring that a man with multiple wives commits adultery unless his first wife has been unfaithful. This challenges societal norms and strips away liberties, igniting outrage among the self-righteous.

In his teachings, Jesus restores equality between husbands and wives, proclaiming that adultery occurs even in the heart and emphasizing the unity of marriage. The Pharisees' incredulous response reflects their hardened hearts, unable to grasp the radical equality Jesus brings.

Moreover, Jesus affirms the validity of singleness for the sake of service, countering the prevailing cultural expectation of marriage and procreation. His words redefine the purpose of marriage and affirm the intrinsic value of each individual, regardless of marital status or lineage.

The woman's main function and value should not be in the role of childbearing.

What?

CHAPTER SEVEN

Jesus and the Spark for Women

Indeed, the teachings of Jesus must have ignited a spark of hope and liberation in the hearts of women everywhere. For centuries, they had been bound by societal norms and patriarchal structures, but Jesus came with a message of equality and dignity for all.

As the Samaritan woman encountered Jesus at the well, she must have been filled with awe and wonder. Here was the man who spoke with authority, who challenged cultural norms, and who offered a glimpse of a new way of life. In his presence, she likely felt a sense of validation and empowerment, knowing that she was valued and respected as an individual.

Jesus' revelation of his identity to her would have been a moment of profound significance. It was not just a meeting between two individuals, but a divine encounter that transformed her perception of herself and her place in the world. She would have marveled at the realization that she was known and loved by the Messiah himself, and that her life had a purpose beyond what she had ever imagined.

In that moment, the Samaritan woman experienced a taste of the freedom and fulfillment that Jesus offered to all who would believe in him. And as she went forth to share her testimony with others, she became a living testament to the life-changing power of encountering Jesus Christ.

Transformative Love: Jesus' Message of Equality and Service

The courtship between the bride and groom is indeed a beautiful symbol of the relationship between Jesus and his church. It's a love story filled with passion, sacrifice, and ultimately, redemption. Jesus gave his life for the church without reservation, demonstrating his unwavering commitment and deep affection.

As we reflect on this profound symbolism, we can't help but be moved by the depth of Jesus' love for his bride. He is coming back for her with all his glory and power, ready to defend and protect her from any harm. It's a powerful reminder of the sacrificial love that every husband should have for his wife, putting her needs and well-being above his own.

Throughout his ministry, Jesus often confronted the religious leaders and those in positions of authority, challenging them to live up to the standards of righteousness and justice. However, there is no record of Jesus addressing women in a harsh or condemning manner. Instead, he consistently uplifted and empowered them, offering them dignity, respect, and compassion.

The impact of Jesus' teachings on women was profound, paving the way for greater equality and opportunity within the early Christian community. As the gospel spread throughout the world, it brought about a transformation in societal attitudes towards women, challenging cultural norms and traditions.

In Matthew 19:13-15, Jesus emphasizes the importance of nurturing and guiding children in the ways of faith. He reminds fathers of their responsibility to lead their children in righteousness, ensuring their spiritual well-being and growth.

In verses 27-30 of the same chapter, Jesus speaks of the reversal of status in his kingdom, where the first will be last and the last will be first. This metaphorical language highlights the value of humility and service in the kingdom of God, challenging the worldly notion of status and power.

Finally, in Matthew 20:20-28, Jesus teaches his disciples about true greatness in the kingdom of God. He encourages them to aspire to greatness, but not through seeking power or status. Instead, true greatness is found in humble service and self-sacrifice, following the example set by Jesus himself.

Overall, the teachings of Jesus challenge us to reevaluate our priorities and values, emphasizing the importance of love, humility, and service in our relationships with one another. It's a message that continues to inspire and guide us today, reminding us of the transformative power of Christ's love and grace.

Rediscovering the True Essence of Community: Restoring Koinonia

Throughout the Gospels and the New Testament, Jesus frequently used household metaphors to convey profound spiritual truths. From the relationship between husband and wife to the care of children, Jesus redefined societal norms and emphasized the importance of equality, love, and service within the household of faith.

In the book of Mark, as well as in Matthew and Luke, Jesus portrays the household in various functions, highlighting the inclusive nature of his message. He refers to his disciples as "brothers and sisters," emphasizing the familial bond among believers. Moreover, Jesus expands the concept of family to include all who do the will of God, referring to them as "children of God" and acknowledging God as the Heavenly Father.

Jesus's teachings and parables often revolved around the dynamics of the household. Whether illustrating the sowing of seed, the laborers in the vineyard, or the faithful steward, Jesus used familiar household scenarios to convey spiritual truths. In doing so, he emphasized the role of every believer within the household of faith, with God as the ultimate Paterfamilias.

However, the concept of koinonia, often translated as "fellowship," has evolved over time. In the New Testament, koinonia referred to joint participation in activities, emphasizing communal effort and shared labor. This sense of fellowship was most vividly experienced within the context of the household, where families worked together in agriculture and craftsmanship.

Today, the traditional household structure has been largely disrupted, and the concept of koinonia has become distorted. Instead of joint participation and shared labor, modern society often prioritizes individualism and personal agendas. The church, once a symbol of communal unity, has become institutionalized, with individuals seeking to meet their own needs and desires.

In light of these changes, there is a need to rediscover the true essence of community and restore koinonia within the household of faith. Just as Jesus challenged societal norms and redefined relationships within the household, so too must believers strive for genuine fellowship, mutual support, and shared responsibility. By embracing the spirit of koinonia, we can recapture the essence of true Christian community and experience the life-changing power of unity and love.

Revisiting the Household of God

As we delve deeper into the study of the New Testament and the letters to the churches, it becomes apparent that the household metaphor plays a significant role in understanding the context of these writings. By recognizing the cultural significance of the household in antiquity and the use of household metaphors by the authors of the New Testament, we gain valuable insight into the message conveyed.

The Word of God takes on new depth and relevance when viewed through this lens. God, in his infinite wisdom, chose to speak directly to the hearts of the people within the societal framework in which they lived. His words, spoken centuries ago, still resonate with profound meaning and relevance today. As a woman, I am particularly struck by the way in which Christ's teachings liberated women and affirmed their dignity and worth. It is truly awe-inspiring to witness the transformative power of his love and grace.

Moving forward, we will explore some of the controversial passages found in the letters to the churches that I think every woman should know. It is important to approach these passages with humility and a willingness to understand the cultural and historical context in which they were written. By doing so, we can gain a deeper understanding of the message intended by the authors and apply it to our lives in a meaningful and relevant way.

Chapter Seven Summary

This chapter was rich in detail and left us so much to chew on and remember. So much to take hold of. I can really appreciate all the more the strong and powerful words of Jesus. What a privilege to look at it so closely, and to have understanding in it.

Women were elevated in position and told that the most important thing they could do in life was to follow and learn from Jesus, to take up his yoke. At the cross, we read that only the Apostle John was present, along with the women. And it was amongst these that Jesus appeared first after his resurrection, giving them the new duty to spread the gospel.

The journey for me just keeps getting more exciting, liberating, and full of good news. I am really beginning to see the bigger picture of the work God was doing. By picturing the different types of households and living environments, and understanding the status and the role of the paterfamilias, I can comprehend the weight of Jesus' words and the different responses from the men, women, and slaves.

Too often, I have felt God was acting blind and not seeing the suffering around him. He was being too silent. Rather, he has nothing to worry about; he had, and has, it all under control. Nothing in the course of time has taken him by surprise.

From Christ's example, the moral law was altered. We can comprehend the raw meaning of koinonia and put it into practice. We can embrace and use liberty better.

Study questions for chapter seven:

1. What is fascinating about the lifestyle of the Jews in antiq-

uity?

2. Is there any symbolism here or anything that remains in culture today?

3. Why has Jesus changed the moral law?

4. Does the church today practice koinonia?

5. How can the church and believers apply koinonia in daily life?

6. How has Jesus' example had an impact?

7. Should it be the personal goal of believers to seek status in the Kingdom of Jesus?

Key points from chapter seven:

- Most households contained fewer than ten people.
- Mortality was high.
- The typical house was made of clay and straw with three rooms over two levels.
- With the mild climate, most activities took place outdoors.
- The wealthy Romans began to live in rural villas outside of the villages, owning a lot of land and having households with as much as 200 people.
- They had servants to tend their fields and landlords to tend their houses.
- Jesus changed the moral law to state that even men cannot marry once divorced.

- Jesus makes the wife an equal partner.
- Jesus was hated by the powerful men because of his words.
- Jesus was ready to lay down his life for the status he mandated.
- Koinonia means more than fellowship; it means brothers and sisters working alongside each other.

Closing prayer for chapter seven:

"Abba, thank You for showing me so much! Thank You for liberating my heart and my mind and for lifting the weight. Thank You for giving me something better to hold onto. The life of Christ was perfect. There were no wasted words and no wasted steps. Thank You for reversing the status to make the last first. To give us all importance. Thank You that my identity is in You. May I wear it well. May those around me see it and be blessed. Amen."

Chapter Eight

The Church and the Woman; the Woman and the Man

C *ast off all bonds of prejudice and custom, and let the love of Christ, which is in you, have free course to run out in all conceivable schemes and methods of labor for the souls of men.* —Catherine Booth

In my journey through life, I have experienced numerous challenges and upheavals that have tested my strength and resilience. From childhood upheavals to personal tragedies, I have faced adversity head-on, relying on my faith in Christ to guide me through the darkest times. As I reflect on my experiences and the peace I have found amidst the storms, I am compelled to share my story in the hopes of inspiring others to find solace and strength in their own faith journey.

Finding Peace in the Storm

Growing up, my life was marked by constant movement and change. My mother's frequent relocations meant that my sister and I were constantly uprooted, never settling in one place for long. Despite the instability, I learned to adapt and find stability within myself through my faith in Christ.

At a young age, I experienced profound loss and tragedy. From losing everything multiple times before the age of 17 to surviving a near-fatal car accident, I endured heartbreak and physical scars that shaped my outlook on life. Through these trials, I learned the importance of resilience and the power of God's grace to carry me through the darkest of times.

Throughout my life, I have faced numerous battles for my physical and emotional well-being, as well. From navigating hurtful relationships to working in the high-stress environment of a hospital emergency room, I have confronted adversity with courage and faith. Each challenge has strengthened my resolve and deepened my trust in God's sovereignty.

In the midst of life's storms, I have discovered a profound sense of peace that transcends understanding. Through my faith in Christ, I have learned to surrender my worries and fears, trusting in God's plan for my life. Despite the trials and tribulations, I have found solace in knowing that God is always in control, guiding me with love and grace.

As I look back on my journey, I am filled with gratitude for the faithfulness of God. Despite the hardships and struggles, I have emerged stronger and more resilient than ever before. My hope is that my story will serve as a beacon of hope for others facing their own trials, reminding them that they are never alone and that there is always hope in Christ.

Perseverance Amidst Adversity

As we delve deeper into the letters to the churches, it's crucial to recall the dynamics of relationships within the culture, particularly the bond between siblings, which held the highest level of trust and the least separation in status. This understanding will provide valuable insight into the strong imagery used in these letters regarding brothers.

It's important to remember that the early churches met in homes, not grand, expensive buildings. Moreover, being a Christian was a crime punishable by death until the fourth century, under the rule of Constantine, when Christianity was legalized. Consequently, the concept of "going to church" as we understand it today was foreign to them—they were the church, meeting in courtyards within larger homes or in rural villas, all part of the same household. This sheds new light on the potential size of the household in Acts when Paul's jailer and his entire household were saved.

Despite facing persecution and being derided by mainstream society as a cult, the first-century church saw its numbers increasing daily. This growth was a testament to the radical transformation brought about by the new status code, which liberated women, blessed children, and elevated slaves from mere property. Known as "The Way," the church was learning to live out its faith amidst adversity.

However, this newfound strength also made the church a threat to society, attracting crafty individuals seeking to manipulate the vulnerable flock. This challenge was a common thread among most local bodies, setting the stage for the issues addressed in the letters to the churches.

Grace and Society: Navigating Status in the Early Church

In his writings, Paul emphasizes the concept of grace, known as "charis" in Greek, to illustrate what God has done for humanity through Jesus. This term was originally used to denote the good deeds of a patron towards a client, establishing and enhancing social status. Similarly, believers are seen as clients of Christ, with Jesus bridging the gap between God and humanity through his life, death, and resurrection.

Psalm 49:7-8 underscores the impossibility of human redemption, highlighting the costly nature of soul ransom. Christ's sacrificial act becomes paramount, surpassing any earthly wealth or effort. As clients of Christ, believers elevate Jesus to the highest status, yet emulate his example of treating others with humility and respect.

In the context of societal norms, the worship of mystic goddesses like Aphrodite, particularly prevalent in Corinth, posed challenges for early Christians. Corinth served as a hub for Aphrodite's worship, with temple prostitution and sensuous practices prevalent. Wealthy women, influenced by these customs, began adopting similar behaviors, prompting concern within the church and Jewish communities.

The issue extended beyond gender, as men also engaged in behaviors deemed inappropriate by Christian and Jewish standards. These cultural clashes raised questions about compromise and maintaining spiritual integrity within a society at odds with Christian values.

CHAPTER EIGHT

Understanding the Metaphorical Use of 'Head' in Scripture

Before delving further into controversial passages, it's crucial to grasp the nuanced meaning of the term "head" as used in Scripture. While it can refer literally to the anatomical head, its metaphorical usage demands deeper exploration.

In contemporary Western interpretation, "head" often connotes authority and dominance, shaping doctrines that dictate male leadership. However, within Greco-Roman culture, the metaphorical understanding of "head" differs significantly.

Scholars like Kruse Kronicle argue against the simplistic interpretation of "head" as denoting authority, advocating for a broader understanding of its metaphorical significance. Rather than the center of rational thought, as in Western culture, Greek and Hebrew anthropology locate reason and emotion in the heart.

Drawing from ancient philosophical and mythological sources, the metaphorical use of "head" aligns more closely with concepts of origin or source. Philosophers like Aristotle and Artemidorus viewed the head as the source of life and light, while Greek mythology depicts creation emerging from the head of deities.

By interpreting passages with "head" metaphorically as "source" or "origin," a new perspective emerges, illuminating the intended meaning of the text. This approach allows for a deeper understanding of the cultural context and the author's intentions, shedding light on contentious passages.

While interpretations may vary, engaging with the metaphorical nuances of "head" enriches our understanding of Scripture and fosters deeper theological reflection.

Here are the verses:

- I Corinthians 11:3, "But I want you to understand that Christ is the head of every man, and the husband is the head of his wife, and God is the head of Christ."
- Ephesians 1:22-23, "And he has put all things under his feet and has made him the head over all things for the church, which is his body, the fullness of him who fills all in all."
- Ephesians 4:15-16, "But speaking the truth in love, we must grow up in every way into him who is the head, into Christ, from whom the whole body, joined and knit together by every ligament with which it is equipped, as each part is working properly, promotes the body's growth in building itself up in love."
- Ephesians 5:22-23, "Wives, be subject to your husbands as you are to the Lord. For the husband is the head of the wife just as Christ is the head of the church, the body of which he is the Savior."
- Colossians 1:18, "He is the head of the body, the church; He is the beginning, the firstborn from the dead so that he might come to have first place in everything."
- Colossians 2:9-10, "For in him the whole fullness of deity dwells bodily, and you have come to fullness in him, who is the head of every ruler and authority."
- Colossians 2:18-19, "Do not let anyone disqualify you, insisting on self-abasement and worship of angels, dwelling on visions, puffed up without cause by a human way of thinking, and not holding fast to the head, from which the whole body, nourished and held together by its ligaments and sinews, grows with a growth that is from God."
- 1 Peter 2:6-7, "For it stands in scripture: 'See, I am laying in Zion a stone, a cornerstone chosen and precious, and whoever

believes in him will not be put to shame.' To you then who believe, he is precious; but for those who do not believe, 'The stone that the builders rejected has become the very head of the corner ...'"

Redefining Authority: A Paradigm Shift in Understanding 1 Corinthians 6

The research from scholars like Kruse has prompted a significant shift in my understanding of key passages, particularly in 1 Corinthians 6. In this chapter, Paul addresses issues of sexual immorality within the Corinthian church, urging believers to flee from such practices. However, the cultural context of the time sheds new light on Paul's message.

In Greco-Roman society, patriarchy was deeply ingrained, with men holding supreme authority within the household. Prostitution was rampant, and mistresses were commonplace among men. Against this backdrop, Paul's admonition against sexual immorality takes on added significance.

Paul challenges the patriarchal system by asserting that the church is owned by Christ, not by men. By transferring authority from men to Christ, Paul disrupts the established power dynamics. This redefinition of authority underscores the radical nature of Christ's teachings, which called for a departure from societal norms.

Furthermore, Paul's emphasis on sexual purity and the sanctity of marriage reflects Christ's relationship with his bride, the church. This symbolism highlights the sacredness of sexual union and underscores the need for believers to honor it.

However, Paul's message likely met resistance from some

men who were accustomed to wielding authority within the household. The heightened moral standards set by Christ presented a challenge, raising the cost of discipleship.

As we delve deeper into these passages, it becomes clear that Paul's teachings were not merely addressing individual sins but were challenging the prevailing cultural norms and redefining authority within the Christian community.

Equality and Harmony in Marriage: Unveiling 1 Corinthians 7

In 1 Corinthians 7, Paul delves into the intricacies of marriage, challenging prevailing cultural norms and advocating for equality and harmony within marital relationships. Verses 1-16 offer profound insights into the dynamics of husband-wife relationships in ancient society.

Paul begins by emphasizing the equality of spouses in the marriage bed, a departure from the traditional view of male dominance. He asserts that both husband and wife have authority over each other's bodies, highlighting the mutual responsibility to honor and respect one another's sexual needs.

Moreover, Paul addresses the prevalent issue of divorce in Greco-Roman culture, urging Christians to prioritize harmony and reconciliation in their marriages. He admonishes both husbands and wives for withholding intimacy and emphasizes the sanctity of the marital bond.

Interestingly, Paul acknowledges the agency of widows and believers married to unbelievers, granting them the right of self-determination. This departure from cultural norms empowers individuals to make decisions based on their own convictions rather than societal expectations.

Furthermore, Paul challenges the hierarchical structure of the church, asserting the equality of believers as siblings in Christ. By leveling the status order, Paul emphasizes the spiritual bond shared by all believers, with Christ as the ultimate authority.

In essence, 1 Corinthians 7 presents a revolutionary perspective on marriage and relationships, advocating for equality, harmony, and mutual respect within the context of Christian community. Paul's teachings transcend cultural norms, offering timeless principles for building strong and fulfilling relationships.

In 1 Corinthians 7:32-35, Paul employs the family metaphor to encourage practical application within the church, promoting unity and equality among believers. His advice challenges prevailing Greek teachings and emphasizes the importance of seeking the counsel of the Lord in all decisions, particularly regarding marriage.

Paul's wisdom extends to the concept of marriage, urging believers to marry in the Lord and seek partners who are equally yoked. He acknowledges the complexities and perils of marriage, advising the church to prioritize spiritual compatibility and seek guidance from God.

Furthermore, Paul addresses the role of parents in considering their children's desires in matters of marriage. By emphasizing the importance of seeking divine counsel, Paul guides the church in making decisions that align with God's will and benefit the body of Christ.

In a broader observation, Paul contrasts worldly wisdom with divine wisdom, cautioning against the pursuit of knowledge for the sake of status. Instead, he emphasizes the importance of wisdom that pleases God, which is foundational for building a strong and harmonious household.

Overall, Paul's teachings in 1 Corinthians 7 offer timeless wisdom on relationships and status, emphasizing the significance of seeking divine guidance and prioritizing spiritual unity within the church community.

Revisiting Controversial Passages: Understanding 1 Corinthians 11 and 14

In 1 Corinthians 11, Paul addresses issues within the public assembly, where worship practices were influenced by both Jewish tradition and the worship of Greek goddesses. He emphasizes modesty and equality between men and women, using the symbolism of head coverings to honor God. Paul underscores the equality of men and women while acknowledging different roles in worship, seeking to maintain order and reverence in gatherings.

Furthermore, in 1 Corinthians 14:34-36, Paul's instructions regarding women's participation in gatherings have been subject to various interpretations. Some theologians suggest later additions to the text, while others view the passage within the context of husband-wife relationships or the cultural dynamics of the time. Regardless, Paul's emphasis on orderly worship and family study of the Word remains relevant.

Amidst controversies and differing interpretations, it's essential to approach these passages with an understanding of their historical context and the principles of interpretation, ensuring a faithful understanding of Paul's teachings.

The inhabitants of Corinth were reputed for their extreme sexual immorality and their depravity. The church in Corinth was divided over many issues.

CHAPTER EIGHT

Paul authored his letters to resolve these problems and to answer questions raised. He addressed concerns regarding marriage and divorce, eating food sacrificed to idols, the conduct of worship, proper use of spiritual gifts, and he advised that all things be done orderly.

In examining 1 Corinthians 14:34-36, scholars have delved into the historical context and textual nuances to understand Paul's instructions regarding women's behavior in gatherings. Some suggest that the prohibition on women speaking may stem from cultural dynamics, such as women's education levels and potential disruptions during worship.

Dr. John Gustavson proposes that Paul may have been quoting Judaizers within the Corinthian church rather than issuing a direct command from the Lord. Gustavson argues that there is no scriptural basis for such a prohibition and suggests that it may have originated from Jewish Oral Law.

Verse 36, following the quoted statement, is interpreted by some as a rebuke or sarcasm directed at the Corinthian men who held restrictive beliefs. Paul's intention may have been to challenge their assumptions rather than enforce silence on women in all circumstances.

Amidst differing interpretations, it's crucial to approach the text with prayerful discernment and an understanding of the broader context. While some may see these verses as limiting women's participation, others emphasize the importance of studying the text comprehensively and allowing the guidance of the Holy Spirit in interpretation.

Chapter Eight Summary

I try to hold onto grace at this point, as a woman. I do want to praise women for their graciousness over the ages. I must keep in mind that it is a fallen world and poor theology has been taught around the globe over the ages. For decades, I trusted the interpretation I was given: women should not teach men, they are inferior. By looking closely at the verses about women in the Pauline books, though, I set off on a journey.

Inferiority and subordination do *not* fall along the lines of equality.

I have long understood that men and women were given different roles, to complete each other, and I take no issues with this. But Paul states that knowledge puffs up. The Greek men sought knowledge and felt superior to the undereducated women. Some of the knowledge gained has not been so beneficial. We've learned it's not the most important thing to seek. Wisdom is, and it's granted by God. This is different from worldly knowledge.

I want to reiterate that even Godly men are affected by the teaching that goes on in the world around them. It is quite obvious to me after breaking down the teaching of Paul that the world was influencing the church, both the Jews and the Greeks.

In this chapter, the most controversial passages, authored by Paul, are unpacked and examined. "Kephale" is defined. Paul addressed men to educate them, stating that not only does the husband own the wife's sexuality, but she owns his. Any owning of people is done by Christ alone. Paul is building up the church and making the status of the people horizontal, brothers and sisters in Christ. He states that we are to live with integrity above the world and include the Lord in our daily decisions.

Study questions for chapter eight:

1. What were the benefits of the church meeting in homes?

2. How could this type of fellowship be more beneficial to believers today than meeting in big buildings?

3. What is the best way to interpret the word "kephale"?

4. What makes Paul's statement that the wife owns the husband's body so profound?

5. What were the believing women doing that was disrupting the church?

6. Do women do this today?

7. How have things changed for women in the Western church today?

Key points from chapter eight:

- Until the fourth century, the church met in homes.
- Early believers did not conceive of "going to church", they *were* the church.
- The first-century church faced persecution and they were mocked by common society and thought to be a cult.
- Paul stresses grace or "charis" in his writings.
- The Temple of Aphrodite in Corinth had more than 1000

prostitutes.
- An entire theology is based on the interpretation of "kephale" to mean women are lesser than men and that a man is in control of the woman.
- Kephale would be better interpreted as "headwaters" or "place of origin".
- Paul teaches to do away with the patriarchal system, stating that it is Christ who does the owning.
- Paul takes away the self-proclaimed right and puts it back in the hands of God, which is the way God intended it.
- Paul states that the husband's sexuality is owned by the wife.
- Paul was urging Christians to separate themselves from the standards of the culture.
- Paul advises the church to seek the counsel of the Lord in their daily decisions.
- Paul addresses some of the issues taking place in the daily assembly.
- When reading the Pauline books, I am only holding one piece of the conversation.

Closing prayer for chapter eight:

CHAPTER EIGHT

"Abba, Your truth is remarkable. Your love unconditional. Thank You for the progress You allow me to make. Thank You for imparting wisdom to me. Thank You for investing in me and setting me apart. May my good deeds represent the Light inside me, and may it be a blessing to those around me. Give me the grace to embrace forgiveness and to overcome some of the bad theology I have been taught. Thank You for the valuable resources which You have made available to me. I only want to seek Your counsel in my daily decisions. It is so wonderful to serve You, my Lord, my Savior, my King. Thank You for such peace. Amen."

Chapter Nine

Making the Bride Beautiful

B*ut I, though I saw and heard these things, refused to write for a long time through doubt and bad opinion and the diversity of human words, not with stubbornness but in the exercise of humility.* —Hildegard of Bingen

Embarking on a journey of humility and learning, I've found profound rewards in exploring diverse creative pursuits, including writing novels, Bible studies, and children's stories. Each endeavor has broadened my perspective and deepened my compassion.

Through writing and studying the Scriptures, I've encountered moments of revelation and awakening. Delving into the New Testament. I've uncovered examples of how Jesus elevated and liberated women, challenging societal norms and advocating for equality.

Examining controversial passages in the Pauline epistles, alongside the cultural context of the time, has provided valuable insights into the challenges faced by early Christian communities. Amidst it all, I've come to understand the ongoing journey of the bride of Christ, striving to maintain purity and readiness for her groom.

In every experience, I've been reminded of the importance of humility, compassion, and continual growth. Through application and reflection, I've found strength and gratitude for the knowledge gained along the way.

Revelations of Equality and Love: Exploring Paul's Epistles

In the journey through Paul's epistles, a profound theme of equality emerges, challenging societal norms and establishing a new understanding of relationships within the church.

Beginning with Galatians, Paul's words echo the Genesis narrative, emphasizing the inherent equality of all humanity as creations in the image of God. In Galatians 3:26-28, Paul further emphasizes this equality, erasing distinctions of status and socio-economic hierarchy. His message resonates particularly with slaves, offering a radical vision of equality that transcends societal norms.

Contrary to some interpretations, Paul does not propagate notions of female inferiority or male dominance. Instead, his teachings in Ephesians 5:22-33 redefine the marital relationship, portraying it as a partnership of mutual respect and sacrificial love. By reimagining the meaning of "head" as life source or origin, Paul challenges traditional patriarchal structures and calls for mutual submission and support within marriage.

As we navigate Paul's teachings, it becomes evident that his message transcends cultural biases and speaks to timeless truths of equality, love, and mutual respect.

Paul's Revolutionary Vision of Marriage

In Paul's epistles, particularly in Ephesians, he unveils a revolutionary vision of marriage that challenges societal norms and patriarchal structures. By redefining the role of the husband as one of sacrificial love and mutual respect, Paul upends traditional notions of dominance and hierarchy within marriage.

Paul emphasizes the importance of husbands loving their wives as they love themselves, recognizing that in marriage, the two become one. This call to sacrificial love is a radical departure from the cultural norms of Paul's time, where the husband held all the power and the wife was dependent on him for her basic needs and legal protection.

Furthermore, Paul's use of the metaphor of the husband as the "head" of the wife is not a directive for dominance, but rather a description of unity and oneness. This concept of unity challenges the prevailing Greco-Roman understanding of household hierarchy, where the paterfamilias held supreme authority.

Paul's teachings on marriage are not only relevant to his time but continue to resonate today, challenging couples to prioritize mutual respect, sacrificial love, and unity in their relationships. As we explore Paul's insights, we discover a profound vision of marriage that transcends cultural boundaries and speaks to the timeless truths of love and equality.

Paul established the importance of first being connected to Christ. Only then could the status of the body be altered and animated. Paul purposely mixed the metaphors of "head and body" and "two become one" to relate the husband and wife to Christ and the church. The common problems between men and women were to be resolved. There was to be mutual submission because the unit was one; because the unit was one there was to be mutual submission. The husband laid down his power and made a sacrifice; the wife had equal status and choose to serve her husband. Both ends glorified God and were useful in his kingdom. It may not have looked very different from the outside, but what happened inside in the mind and the heart bred a different result than relationships in the world. It was a union empowered by love.

In Paul's view, the husband's willingness to prioritize his wife's well-being and to sacrificially love her as he loves himself is the catalyst for a fundamental shift in the relationship dynamic. No longer does the husband wield unilateral authority; instead, he is called to relinquish his self-interest and to prioritize the unity and flourishing of the marriage partnership.

This paradigm shift not only challenges societal expectations but also serves as a powerful witness to the transformative power of love. Unbelieving observers are confronted with a radical alternative to the prevailing cultural norms of dominance and exploitation. As they witness the warmth and mutual respect between husband and wife, they are drawn to the light of Christ shining through their relationship.

Moreover, Paul's vision for marriage has far-reaching implications beyond individual relationships. It serves as a beacon of hope in a world marked by division and selfishness. As couples embrace Paul's teachings and embody sacrificial love in their marriages, they become agents of transformation, spreading the message of Christ's love and unity to a world in desperate need of redemption.

Ultimately, Paul's vision for marriage is not merely a personal or relational matter; it is a revolutionary force that has the power to reshape entire societies and bring about lasting change. Through the transformative power of love, marriages become a testament to the reconciling and redeeming work of Christ, drawing others into the abundant life found in him.

Unpacking Foundational Teachings in Colossians and Timothy

The book of Colossians delivers groundbreaking mandates, urging believers to submit, show sensitivity, obedience, and recognize their ultimate service to the Lord Jesus Christ. In Colossians 3:18-4:4, Paul articulates the significance of Christ's sacrificial love for his bride, the Church, inspiring believers to emulate his example through prayer and faithful living.

Reflecting on the obedience and understanding demonstrated by the early church, one is humbled and inspired by their commitment to God's purpose. By imparting wisdom upon Paul, God illuminated the path to redemption, extending salvation beyond the Jewish community to all peoples, as intended from the outset.

Transitioning to the cultural context of the writing of 1 Timothy, one must understand the emergence of Gnosticism, marked by the worship of a feminine deity and various deviant practices. In addressing the widows in 1 Timothy, Paul counters the influence of these cults, cautioning against false teachings spread by wealthy women enamored with Gnostic practices. The expression "fight the good fight" resonates with Paul's admonition to combat such falsehoods, drawing from Hellenistic moral philosophy.

Timothy's charge in Ephesus takes on added significance against the backdrop of the renowned Temple of Diana, emphasizing the spiritual battle against idolatry and false doctrines prevalent in the region.

In fact, Ephesus was home to some of the most magnificent buildings in Asia Minor. It held the largest outdoor theater in the world with a capacity of 50,000. And the most influential orators and philosophers of this time gathered to speak in Ephesus. Ironically, today only one pillar remains from the 140 pillars that it took to erect the temple. The rest were leveled in an earthquake and their ruins were carried away and used to build the Basilica of St. John nearby.

In delving into the depths of understanding Scripture, it becomes imperative to confront even the most contentious passages, such as 1 Timothy 2:8-15. Often, these sections are approached with trepidation or glossed over with preconceived notions. However, a thorough examination is necessary to grasp the intended message, especially concerning the role of women in the early Christian context.

The passage in question, I Timothy 2:8-15, has sparked varied interpretations throughout history. While some may assert a rigid interpretation implying women's silence and submission, it is crucial to challenge such dogmatic readings. Rather than succumbing to a simplistic understanding, we are called to engage with the text deeply and critically, seeking a more nuanced comprehension of its significance.

As we embark on this exploration, let us set aside preconceptions and approach the passage with an open mind and a commitment to uncovering its true meaning within its historical and cultural context. Only through diligent study and reflection can we discern the timeless wisdom and relevance contained within these verses.

Challenging Misconceptions: Understanding Gender Dynamics in Scripture

Throughout history, misconceptions regarding the trustworthiness and roles of men and women have permeated societal and religious frameworks. The narrative that Eve's deception renders all women untrustworthy is one such fallacy that requires careful scrutiny. Instead, as Paul asserts in Romans 3:4, the ultimate trust lies with God, with every individual - regardless of gender - prone to fallibility.

Moreover, the prevalence of deception within the church, often perpetrated by men, underscores the folly of assigning inherent trustworthiness based on gender. The insidious influence of false teaching, reminiscent of the Nicolaitans' format, has persisted, threatening the authenticity of Christian fellowship.

Interpreting passages like 1 Timothy 2:8-15 demands contextual sensitivity and an avoidance of imposing contemporary biases onto ancient texts. The revolutionary nature of early Christian fellowship, where men and women congregated together, likely necessitated practical guidelines to maintain order and prevent external influences from infiltrating the community.

CHAPTER NINE

Rather than endorsing male dominance, these instructions likely aimed to foster harmony and guard against the infiltration of pagan practices. Thus, dismissing the context and cultural nuances risks distorting the intended message and perpetuating harmful interpretations.

Ultimately, a nuanced understanding of Scripture requires diligent study, humility, and a commitment to upholding the principles of love, equality, and mutual respect within the body of believers. Only through such discernment can we transcend ingrained biases and embrace the fullness of God's truth.

In dissecting 1 Timothy 2:8-15, it becomes evident that Paul's underlying aim is to combat false teachings and maintain peace within the fellowship. Despite the passage's contentious nature, a nuanced examination reveals insights crucial for understanding the role of women in the early church.

Paul's deliberate addressing of men before women underscores his emphasis on maintaining order and sound teaching within the community. Notably, his frequent admonitions to the women in the Ephesian church indicate the significance he placed on their adherence to correct doctrine.

Central to interpreting this passage is the Greek term *authentein*, which poses challenges due to its unique usage. Rather than simply denoting authority, it encompasses broader connotations, including the potential for usurpation or domination. Thus, the passage's meaning hinges on understanding the nuanced relationship between teaching and authority.

While traditional translations may imply restrictions on women's involvement in ministry, a closer examination suggests a more balanced interpretation. The prohibition may pertain to women seizing authority in an aggressive or domineering manner rather than a blanket prohibition on teaching or leadership roles.

In essence, navigating the complexities of 1 Timothy 2:8-15 requires a nuanced understanding of language, context, and cultural dynamics. Rather than imposing rigid interpretations, it behooves us to approach the passage with humility, recognizing its potential for diverse meanings and interpretations. Ultimately, the overarching message remains one of maintaining peace, sound doctrine, and mutual respect within the body of Christ.

Indeed, interpretations of the term "saved" (*sozo*) in 1 Timothy 2:15 vary, and some argue for a more literal understanding, suggesting that it pertains to physical safety during childbirth. According to this interpretation, Paul may be conveying the idea that women who conduct themselves in a peaceable and humble manner will be granted protection and deliverance from harm during the childbirth process.

However, this interpretation poses theological challenges and raises questions about the implications for women who experience complications or difficulties during childbirth despite their faith and behavior. To assert that every woman's pregnancy outcome is directly correlated with her level of faith or conduct can lead to problematic conclusions, such as attributing adverse outcomes to divine punishment or neglect.

It's essential to approach this interpretation with caution and recognize the limitations of applying such a literal understanding universally. Instead, we might view Paul's words in a broader context, acknowledging the cultural and theological nuances at play. Rather than offering a blanket promise of physical safety, Paul may be emphasizing the spiritual significance of childbirth within the narrative of salvation history, highlighting the redemptive role of Mary in bearing

Christ.

Ultimately, interpreting this passage requires humility and sensitivity to the diverse experiences of women. While exploring various interpretations can deepen our understanding of the text, we must avoid rigid interpretations that oversimplify complex issues and fail to account for the realities of human suffering and God's mysterious ways.

Navigating Cultural Influences in Greco-Roman Society

During the Greco-Roman period, women often turned to deities like Artemis or Isis for protection during childbirth. It's possible that Paul's reference in his writings could be an encouragement for women to turn to Jesus instead of these pagan practices.

Considering Paul's other letters, the cultural context of the churches he addressed, and historical evidence of women serving as apostles and prophetesses in the 1st century, it's difficult to conclude that women were universally barred from positions of authority within the church. Additionally, the presence of women deacons suggests a more nuanced understanding of women's roles in the early church.

However, in Ephesus, where the church was influenced by Gnosticism and the societal shift towards greater freedom for women, Paul's exhortation for women to pursue holiness, marriage, and childbearing may have been a response to the teachings of the Gnostic movement, which discouraged these practices as a means of attaining spiritual enlightenment.

Paul's mention of Eve in his writings is not an indictment of all women but rather an acknowledgment of the ongoing spiritual battle against deception and false teaching. By stressing hope in Eve's salvation, Paul underscores the importance of remaining rooted in truth amidst the challenges of the contemporary church, particularly in combating false doctrines prevalent in the Ephesian community.

Therefore, the interpretation of Paul's instructions in 1 Timothy must be contextualized within the broader theme of combating false teaching rather than serving as a blanket prohibition against women's participation in church leadership or teaching roles. Misapplication of this passage has led to harmful consequences in the contemporary church, underscoring the need for careful and informed biblical interpretation.

Navigating Church Leadership and Roles

In II Timothy 2:25-26, the directive to correct those led astray with gentleness aligns with the overarching theme of combating false teaching within the church. This emphasis on correction precedes the conclusion of Paul's letter to Timothy, underscoring its significance in maintaining doctrinal integrity.

A brief glance at I Timothy 3:1-13 reveals the delineation of various positions within the church body. It's crucial to interpret these instructions within their historical context, considering the societal norms and roles prevalent at the time. While men held prominent positions in society, Paul's guidance to Timothy aimed at maintaining a distinct and morally upright witness to the world.

Interpreting these passages requires caution against reading contemporary cultural norms into the text or inferring meanings that aren't explicitly stated. For instance, the requirement for men to have only one wife doesn't mandate marriage but rather emphasizes marital fidelity. Moreover, the inclusion of qualifications for women in verse eleven likely points to the role of women deacons, reflecting Paul's broader aim of ensuring well-informed and discerning leadership within the church.

It's essential to recognize the egalitarian nature of Paul's teachings, which emphasize equality and mutual respect within the body of Christ. Examples of prominent women in leadership roles, such as Junia, Priscilla, Phoebe, Nympha, and Lydia, challenge traditional gender roles and highlight the diverse contributions of women in the early church.

In reflecting on these passages, it's crucial to uphold the principles of inclusivity and recognition of women's leadership and teaching roles within the church, as demonstrated by Paul's affirmations of their contributions to the body of Christ. Moreover, linguistic nuances, such as the gender-neutral translation of names, underscore the need for careful interpretation to capture the full breadth of Paul's teachings.

Understanding Societal Transitions in Early Christianity

The journey through early Christianity offers invaluable insights into the radical societal transitions catalyzed by Christ and the pioneering efforts of the early church. These transitions reshaped norms and challenged established hierarchies, particularly regarding the roles and status of women.

Christ's teachings and interventions underscored the accountability of men in governing with respect and consideration for the welfare of all individuals. The transformative impact of these principles spurred societal changes that were revolutionary for their time.

Furthermore, gaining a nuanced understanding of the daily lives of women in antiquity enriches our appreciation of their experiences and challenges. By delving into historical contexts, we gain perspective on the cultural dynamics that influenced women's roles and opportunities within society.

As we continue our exploration of the New Testament, we encounter ongoing controversies surrounding women within the church, shedding light on the complexities of navigating gender dynamics in early Christian communities.

Chapter Nine Summary

It is with a humble heart that I approach the Word of God. By giving these controversial texts a deeper look, by understanding the culture of the day and the challenges that the church was facing, I better conceive what Paul was trying to convey. I certainly don't expect my opinion to be popular. And I don't expect to impact the entire body of Christ; however, I do hope to impact some of those that have had the same questions and the same battles that I have had. I have peace of mind in what I write.

Nearly every church that was being planted from the start had to fight against false teaching. That is exactly why Paul says he "fought the good fight" in the book II Timothy. It would seem the wealthy women within the body had too much time and too much worldly knowledge. They were heavily influenced by other women of high status in society in word, deed, and manner of dress. It would also seem that they were then seizing authority over their leaders and spreading false teaching like a disease. Paul warns against this. We must keep in mind we are only holding one piece of an entire conversation that has been taking place.

Study questions for chapter nine:

1. How could the early church impact society with the status code erased within it?

2. What are some of the unique ways Paul has used symbolism in his texts?

3. Why does Paul address men first in his texts?

4. What was Paul referring to when he said he "fought the good fight"?

5. What is perhaps the best way to translate what Paul was saying when he wrote that a woman must not seize authority over a man?

6. Does redefining what Paul is saying give a different perspective regarding a woman having authority within the church?

7. Is it possible for a woman today to really have authority the way religion has been organized?

Key points from chapter nine:

- Equality is on the rise in Galatians with the doing away of status within the church.
- Paul uses unique symbolism in his texts.
- Paul purposefully mixes the metaphors of "head" and

"body" and "two become one" to relate to the husband and wife and Christ and the church.
- Paul suggests the husband lay down his power and make a sacrifice; the wife should respond by choosing to serve her husband.
- During the time of Timothy, Gnosticism was finding its way in the church.
- Some of the wealthy women in the church were influenced by the Isis cult.
- "Fight the good fight" was borrowed from Hellenistic moral philosophy and was implied in the battle against false teaching.
- The better translation of I Timothy 2:8-15 is that a woman may not seize authority from a man in authority; she should be peaceable.
- To cut and paste this passage has proven destructive within the body.
- The church was trying to maintain certain facets within to reach the world it was separated from.

Closing prayer from chapter nine:

CHAPTER NINE

"Abba, Thank You for choosing to open up your word before me. Thank You for giving me an understanding of some very controversial passages. They can be overwhelming to read and difficult to comprehend. I want to be a beacon of hope to others that are struggling with the interpretation of these passages. Please direct me always toward the truth. I desire that Your bride be whole and ready for You to claim her. Please strengthen her. For You have made all things new. Thank You. Amen."

Chapter Ten

The Silence of Women

There are two ways of spreading light: to be the candle or the mirror that reflects it. —Edith Wharton

---

Living amidst the picturesque mountains of southern Spain, hiking serves as both a pastime and a metaphor for life's journey. Stepping out the front door presents a myriad of trails to explore, each offering its own blend of scents and sights. While I don't mind wandering aimlessly, I find greater fulfillment in having a destination to reach and a fresh route to return by.

Yet, I've learned the hard way that straying from marked paths can lead to challenging terrain and unexpected obstacles.

Much like navigating the trails, my exploration of biblical passages concerning women and authority in the church has been a journey of discovery and growth.

Initially, I didn't intend to write a book on the topic. My goal was simply to align my thinking with biblical principles and overcome the hurdles before me. Along the way, I've encountered passages in the New Testament that shed light on this complex issue, revealing how authors utilized household codes as metaphors to convey deeper spiritual truths.

As I continue to delve into these passages that I think every woman should know, I invite others to join me on this journey of understanding and reflection. Together, let's navigate the path of faith with humility, openness, and a desire to grasp the timeless wisdom contained within Scripture.

Turn now to the book of Titus.

Navigating Truth in Titus: Unpacking Gender Roles and Submission

Delving into the book of Titus, traditionally attributed to the apostle Paul, offers profound insights into the cultural dynamics of the island of Crete and the challenges faced by Titus in his role as a teacher within the burgeoning Christian community. The Cretans were renowned for their licentiousness and a marked lack of submission, exacerbated by the dissemination of false teachings propagated by Jewish rabbis.

The popular saying about Cretans, which originated from the ancient Greek philosopher Epimenides, is famously quoted by the apostle Paul in his letter to Titus. It goes: "Cretans are always liars, evil brutes, lazy gluttons." This saying reflects the negative reputation attributed to the inhabitants of the island of Crete during ancient times.

Titus's mission encompassed guiding various demographic groups within the church, including older men and women, as well as younger men and women (Titus 2:1-6). Within the societal norms of the time, it was deemed culturally unacceptable for a man to instruct young women, necessitating that this role fell upon older women. While the Scriptures do not explicitly forbid women from teaching men, prevailing educational disparities and entrenched societal norms likely precluded such scenarios.

In verse five of Titus 2, Paul underscores the imperative for the body of Christ to live lives that reflect the truth of God's Word, bearing good fruit and epitomizing the grace of God in their conduct. This call to live above reproach mandated a renunciation of worldly desires and a wholehearted embrace of the principles of righteousness.

Of particular note is the concept of submission elucidated in verse five, which was revolutionary in a society characterized by rigid hierarchies and entrenched social stratification. In the context of the Christian community, individuals were afforded the freedom to voluntarily submit themselves, countering societal norms and advancing the gospel message (Titus 2:5).

The concept of submission mentioned in verse five is crucial. In Greek, the word used for "submission" is "hupotassesthai," which conveys the idea of voluntary submission or choosing to place oneself in a lower position. This was a revolutionary concept in the Greco-Roman society of the time, where women, children, and slaves were relegated to lower ranks without any choice in the matter.

Within the body of Christ, however, believers were presented with a new paradigm. They were given the freedom to choose to submit voluntarily, not out of compulsion or societal pressure, but out of a desire to glorify God and advance the message of the gospel. This voluntary submission meant breaking away from the prevailing status codes of society, where social gain and hierarchy were paramount.

Paul's instructions to Titus underscored three significant contrasts to the societal norms of the time. Firstly, believers were urged to reject conformity to the worldly order and prioritize spiritual values over social status. Secondly, the traditional patriarchal structure, where the oldest man ruled the household, was challenged, signaling a shift in authority within Christian households. Finally, every member of the household, regardless of social standing, was granted the freedom to act according to their convictions within the framework of Christian principles.

By envisioning a community where masters honored and cared for their slaves, Paul provided a tangible example of the life-giving power of submission and mutual respect within the body of Christ (Titus 2:9-10).

Paul's instructions to Titus served to challenge the prevailing status quo, advocating for a rejection of worldly status-seeking and promoting mutual respect and submission within the body of Christ. This call to submission was not merely a personal decision but held significant missional implications, ultimately reflecting a profound submission to Christ and God the Father (Titus 2:11-14).

Embracing the Radical Mission: Insights from 1 Peter

In the first chapter of 1 Peter, a foundational mission is laid out for believers, emphasizing their role as priests to intercede for the unsaved world and proclaim God's mighty acts into the darkness. This mission remains urgent and vital for the body of Christ today.

The concept of being chosen by God is profound and empowering, urging believers to live as people set apart for a great work. Peter challenges the chosen to embrace their freedom while willingly submitting to authority—a revolutionary idea in the Greco-Roman society of the time.

A significant aspect of 1 Peter is its audience. In a society where only the paterfamilias was typically addressed, Peter's letter breaks barriers by addressing slaves and women. This inclusivity speaks volumes about the radical nature of the message and its impact on society.

As a recipient of this transformative message, I am keenly aware of the abundant life received through Christ. It is my responsibility to safeguard this life and live it out effectively each day.

Often, the message from the pulpit has focused solely on securing salvation from hell, neglecting the abundant life believers are called to live now. The Kingdom of God is not a distant future reality but a present force within us, guiding us in our daily lives until the return of our Lord.

While my role in heaven may differ, for now, my focus is on succeeding in the work set before me today. My life is missional, and I am called to engage with the darkness around me, proclaiming the imminent return of my Lord and Savior. This is the meaningful work I am privileged to live out each day.

This is what Peter was saying. Lay down our rights, our obsession with status and importance. We must look remarkably different from the world. Christ lived a redemptive life through his suffering; I am to do the same. Submitting to the social order by choice is to bring honor to Jesus. Peter is not justifying slavery or male superiority. The call is missional.

Navigating Social Dynamics: Women in Church Leadership

In contemplating the role of women in church leadership, it's essential to consider the cultural and societal contexts in which we live. In places like England, where women hold prominent leadership positions in both society and the church, the inclusion of women in leadership roles is commonplace and accepted. However, in other regions, such as parts of America, gender norms still heavily influence perceptions of leadership, both in society and within religious institutions.

The concept of ordination, though widely practiced, lacks clear biblical mandate for either men or women. Yet, it remains a significant factor in determining who can assume leadership roles within the church. This discrepancy between cultural norms and biblical principles raises questions about the church's response to societal changes and the promotion of gender equality in leadership.

If we heed the counsel of biblical teachings, particularly those of figures like Peter, we find a call to embrace cultural nuances while remaining true to the gospel message. Peter's emphasis on freedom should not lead to discord with the host culture but rather a strategic engagement that promotes the gospel in diverse contexts.

However, it appears that the church, in many instances, has lagged behind societal progress regarding gender equality in leadership. While the world sees increasing numbers of women in leadership positions across various sectors, the church often lags in mirroring this diversity within its own leadership structures.

Asking for divine wisdom and guidance is paramount in navigating these complex issues. It requires humility to reconsider long-held beliefs and to align our practices with the broader principles of love, justice, and equality espoused in the Scriptures.

Personal growth and transformation, as seen in the shift from opposing to embracing women in leadership, highlight the importance of continual reflection and study. It also challenges us to reevaluate the traditional norms and structures within the church to ensure they align with the inclusive and transformative message of the gospel. Ultimately, our goal should be to create spaces where all individuals, regardless of gender, can contribute their gifts and talents to the work of God's kingdom.

Rethinking Church: Embracing Change and Biblical Equality

As I delved deeper into my studies, I found myself confronted with a startling realization: the traditional Sunday ceremony, as practiced in many churches, seemed to be fundamentally flawed. Instead of fostering growth, participation, and empowerment within the body of Christ, it often left members feeling passive, unfulfilled, and disconnected.

CHAPTER TEN

In my journey of discovery, I began to see that the controversy surrounding women in leadership roles within the church would perhaps not even exist if the church were functioning in a healthier manner. If every member were actively contributing their gifts in smaller, more intimate gatherings, the body would flourish, feeling satisfied, thriving, and useful.

However, the current model of "church" seems to primarily benefit those in positions of authority, while leaving many members feeling marginalized and uninvolved. This is not to say that God is not blessing the church in its current state, but rather to acknowledge that there is potential for greater growth and effectiveness if we are willing to embrace change and seek the guidance of the Holy Spirit.

Reflecting on the wisdom of Peter, I am reminded of his radical experiences and teachings. From his vision of God's acceptance of the Gentiles to Jesus' breaking of societal norms, Peter's life and ministry were marked by a willingness to challenge tradition and embrace the leading of the Holy Spirit.

Yet, in many church assemblies today, the pastor is often elevated to the status of a paterfamilias, overshadowing the equality and diversity that should characterize the body of Christ. This hierarchical structure runs counter to the teachings of Jesus, who emphasized the importance of unity and mutual submission within the body.

While I acknowledge that the prospect of women taking on prominent preaching roles in American megachurches may seem unfamiliar to some, I am not advocating for a "female take-over" or a complete overhaul of traditional practices. Rather, I believe that spiritual growth and healing within the organized church require prayer, devotion, and a willingness to seek God's counsel.

I do not align myself with any particular theological camp or seek to impose my beliefs on others. Instead, I have dedicated myself to thorough research and study, seeking to understand and articulate biblical principles of equality and unity within the body of Christ.

Ultimately, my hope is that my journey of discovery will benefit others and inspire them to deepen their own understanding of their faith. As mature believers, we should be able to defend and articulate our beliefs using biblical principles, striving for unity and effectiveness in advancing the Kingdom of God.

Let's examine one final passage: I Peter 3:1-7.

Embracing God's Design: A Woman's Journey of Understanding

As I reflect on the teachings of Peter regarding the role of women in the church and in society, I am struck by the profound wisdom and insight contained within his words. Peter, in his letters, offers guidance to women on how to conduct themselves in a manner that is pleasing to God and reflects the beauty of a gentle and quiet spirit.

In examining Peter's instructions, I am challenged to evaluate my own life and see if it aligns with the qualities that God values: quietness and gentleness. These characteristics may not always come naturally to me, but they are traits that I aspire to cultivate in my daily life.

Peter's exhortation for women to adorn themselves with a gentle and quiet spirit, rather than focusing solely on outward appearance, serves as a powerful reminder of the importance of inner transformation. It is a call to prioritize the cultivation of inner virtues over external adornment.

CHAPTER TEN

Furthermore, Peter provides women with a significant lineage, comparing them to Sarah, the wife of Abraham, by calling them "daughters of Sarah." This elevates the status of women and emphasizes their importance in God's plan. It is a recognition of their value and contribution to the Kingdom of God. This was the first time such comparisons were made. We are very familiar with the term "sons of Abraham" but to call women "daughters of Sarah" was revolutionary!

Additionally, Peter addresses the dynamics of marriage, encouraging wives to submit to their husbands and honoring them as equal heirs in Christ. This does not diminish the value or worth of women but rather establishes a framework for mutual respect and partnership within marriage.

Moreover, Peter emphasizes the responsibility of husbands to honor and consider their wives, recognizing them as equal heirs and partners in the faith. This challenges the traditional patriarchal norms of society and calls husbands to a higher standard of love and respect for their wives.

In exploring the teachings of Peter and other New Testament authors on the roles of men and women in the church and society, we uncover valuable insights into humility, submission, and mutual respect. These principles guide us in honoring God and reflecting His love to the world around us.

Throughout this journey of study and reflection, it becomes clear that patriarchy was not the agenda of Jesus or the early church. Instead, they offered examples and guidance for living peacefully within patriarchal societies while prioritizing our position in the Kingdom of God.

As we continue to navigate the complexities of gender dynamics, may we embrace these principles and strive to live in harmony with God's design, honoring Him in all our interactions and relationships.

And this leads me to the next question. What unfolded in the church's journey after the close of the New Testament canon?

Chapter Ten Summary

In the Greco-Roman culture, Paul emphasizes the significance of living in Christ, where the relationship between believers mirrors the bond of siblings, unchallenged by status. He provides practical guidance for the church, urging them to maintain God as the ultimate authority figure. Similarly, Peter warns against alienating the church from the world they seek to reach and advises against immature behavior stemming from newfound equality in status.

Both Paul and Peter reject hierarchical structures within the early church, advocating for a horizontal status where love and service are paramount. Paul emphasizes the importance of mutual love and respect between spouses, which extends to the church's impact on society. Peter stresses the importance of maintaining approachability and orderliness, centered on love and consideration for others, to glorify God and attract others to the faith.

The intimate nature of early Christian gatherings, often held in homes, fostered deep bonds among believers. Their commitment to worship and work together created a unique sense of community and unity. Despite the challenges of their time, early Christians prioritized their identity as heirs of Christ over worldly status, exemplified by their selfless acts of service during times of crisis.

In studying the New Testament, we see a consistent theme of prioritizing love, unity, and mission over societal status. This mindset empowered early Christians to prioritize their identity in Christ and demonstrate selfless love in tangible ways, even at great personal risk. Their example challenges us to reevaluate our own priorities and live out our faith authentically in today's world.

Study questions for chapter ten:

1. What was the warning to Titus?

2. Is there any direct statement issued by Paul for women not to teach men?

3. What is Paul encouraging?

4. Why did Paul and Peter teach the believers to choose to be lower in rank?

5. What was the mission God entrusted us with?

6. What was so special about Peter giving women matriarchal lineage to Sarah?

7. Why did the early church have such an impact on their society?

Key points from chapter ten:

- Titus was on the Isle of Crete.
- Cretans were known for their licentious behavior.
- Jewish rabbis were teaching false doctrine and the church

started to also.
- Titus was instructed against teaching single women.
- Paul instructed Titus to teach the church to be above reproach, to be different than the world.
- The church is to be purified to be his people who are zealous to do good works for their Savior.
- Choosing to be submissive is missional.
- Peter is laying the foundation to live by to accomplish the mission we were entrusted with by God.
- The letter from Peter was addressed to slaves and women, who were never addressed by teachers or philosophers.
- Christ lived a redemptive life through his suffering; I am to do the same.
- The whole process of ordination is not biblical.
- Peter did not want my freedom from status to offend the host culture.
- Today I risk doing this if I insist on female subordination in a society that does not.
- Most church assemblies treat the head pastor as paterfamilias and put the status vertical again.
- Peter gives women a matriarchal lineage to Sarah, thus honoring women.
- Peter reminds all that women are equal heirs.
- The early church lived and worshiped together with their whole lives.

CHAPTER TEN

Closing prayer for chapter ten:

"Abba, Thank You for giving such inspiration to the authors of the Bible. Thank You that they were so connected to You, they could hear You without interruption. The world was turned upside down because of their faithfulness. May I be so worthy, Lord? Please continue to give me an understanding of Your Word as the days go. Let me be a part of a body that is sensitive to Your Word. Write Your truth on my heart. Cleanse my heart and my lips that I may be a candle in the darkness. Amen."

Chapter Eleven

After the Testaments

> How wonderful it is that nobody need wait a single moment before starting to improve the world. — Anne Frank

The life of Christ serves as the nexus between the Old and New Testaments, fulfilling the divine plan where the Old Testament is concealed and the New Testament is revealed, according to Augustine's profound insight. As the Bible unfolds, it becomes evident that both sections are intricately connected, forming a cohesive narrative centered on Jesus Christ, whose life transformed the culture of Israel and subsequently influenced cultures worldwide. However, with the advent of the church age following Christ's ascension, the reciprocal interaction between the church and various cultures has shaped the modern landscape of Christianity.

The Evolution of the Church: From Early Principles to Modern Trends

The church has undergone significant changes since its inception, diverging from its early principles outlined by Paul and Peter. While examining guidelines for women's attire and the demise of patriarchy in the church, it becomes apparent that societal trends have heavily influenced contemporary Christianity, much like they did during the early church under the Roman Empire.

In contrast to the early church's respectful and nonconforming approach to societal structures, the modern church often reflects societal norms rather than embodying its distinctive identity. The expectation of Christ's imminent return, prevalent in the early church, seems to have waned, leading to a loss of urgency and mission-driven living among believers.

Comparing the behaviors of the modern church with those of its early counterpart reveals a stark contrast. The urgency and missional focus that characterized the early church have been replaced by complacency and a lack of anticipation for Christ's return.

There is a growing consensus among believers that the church needs to reclaim the household vision of the New Testament era, emphasizing intimacy, familial relationships, and a mission-oriented mindset. However, this revival must transcend mere aesthetics and encompass a fundamental shift in how the church operates and engages with society.

Historically, the church's identity shifted during the fourth century after Christianity's legalization, adopting practices reminiscent of pagan worship and losing the intimacy of home-based gatherings. This shift mirrored broader societal changes, such as the industrialization that separated work from the household, fundamentally altering the church's dynamics.

As we navigate the complexities of modern Christianity, it is essential to reevaluate our priorities and align them with the timeless principles outlined in the New Testament. Only then can the church regain its mission-driven focus and effectively impact society for the glory of God.

The Decline of Missional Living

Today, less than 2 percent of everything consumed in households is produced within the home—a stark contrast to historical self-sufficiency. This shift has led to a detachment from missional living, both in the household and the church. Workplaces have become the primary generators of income, while homes are merely places of consumption and refuge from work-related stress.

In this advanced twenty-first century world, mental illness rates among youths are higher than ever before, and families are increasingly dysfunctional. The decline in family size and the quest for individual identity contribute to this societal upheaval.

Similarly, the modern church has drifted away from its mission-oriented roots. Congregants often attend services seeking emotional support and nurturing, creating a culture of consumption rather than contribution. Pastors bear the burden of surrogate parenthood, leading to burnout and feelings of failure.

Furthermore, the prevalence of entertainment-focused church services perpetuates this cycle, with megachurches bearing significant financial burdens to sustain their operations. However, a growing trend towards underground and grassroots movements suggests a desire for a return to a more authentic, missional expression of faith.

Amidst discussions of the Great Reset and the New Normal, there is speculation about whether the Holy Spirit is guiding believers towards a paradigm shift in preparation for the future. As we navigate these changes, it is essential to reevaluate our priorities and reclaim the missional mandate of the early church. Back in the days of the Temple, under Mosaic Law, there was a Holy of Holies. Only the High Priest could enter, always a man, and only on the Day of Atonement. This was symbolic of Christ. Through him, the final atonement has taken place. Now everyone may enter, women and children and slaves, regardless of their status.

There are practices within Christianity today that have come down to us over the centuries since its legalization that we might do well without. But somewhere along the line, Christianity was "organized" and this is the way the bishops sought to go about the business. I'm too far removed to understand if it's the best way to do things, or it's even God's intent. But if it isn't, he's allowing it because he is working around it, and able to see his agenda through. In other words, it's serving a purpose. There are some things under this umbrella that I think are worth knowing, and I will simplify them because the topics are dry and heady.

It all starts with clergy. The understanding I have today of *clergy* is that it refers to a special, separate group of people leading me in my "spiritual worship." In contrast, the biblical "clergy" are one group as defined by the Greek word *kleros* meaning *lot* or *inheritance*. Figuratively speaking, then, all believers represent the clergy, the "inheritance of God."

Furthermore, the adjective *laikos,* meaning *of the common people,* is neither in the New Testament nor in the Old. Around 300 BC, it was an adjective used to reference the rural people in Egypt regarding some of the perverse things they did. It was a common synonym for the word *bebelos* meaning *profane* or *unholy.* Earlier than 100 AD, a letter was written to the church in Corinth by Clement of Rome exhorting the "common people" to preserve the Godly order, addressing the duties of those who were neither priest nor Levite, calling them *laymen.* The reference is I Clement 40:5 and this is the first known use of the word *laikos* in the church.

Around the second century, the word was commonly used to reference *idiotes* or *unprofessionals* in Greek literature. And, yes, it is where the contemporary word *idiot* has derived. By the third and fourth centuries, laikos made its way into the Christian vocabulary and over time it evolved into the word *laity* to reference unprofessional, common, and profane people as opposed to the educated, holy, and sacred "clergy." This is where a major division began within Christianity, separating the people once again into statuses, giving the leaders higher ground.

Today this separation remains, and in many churches, the mentality is that any "real ministering" is done by the special "clergy" supposedly given an extra portion of spirituality. And any assistance clergy may need is fulfilled by "laity" or "idiots and unprofessionals." During the Reformation, this problem of special "clergy" was addressed. Those with authority dealt with it by elevating certain laity. These part-time workers assisted the full-time workers as needed. They could not administer the sacraments; they didn't have a degree from a seminary; they were not on the payroll; they didn't have a special title; they were engaged mostly with "secular" things.

But this brought further division because instead of a two-tiered ladder there were then three.

Nonetheless, this system stuck and remains the same even up to today.

Overcoming Dualism and Sexism

Scripture teaches that all believers are part of the clergy, representing the body of God. However, in certain churches, dualism and sexism have infiltrated, undermining the true essence of the church. There is a prevailing belief that laity and women are not to be entrusted with sacred duties, relegating them to secondary roles in the church's ministry.

Upon examining the New Testament, it becomes evident that Paul envisioned leaders like Titus and Timothy as coaches rather than exclusive rulers. The church requires leadership, but the current division between clergy and laity, and men and women, feels burdensome instead of light as Jesus promised in Matthew 11:28. Christ came to free us from the constraints of the Mosaic Law (Acts 13:39), calling for a return to the early vision of the church where every member functioned as clergy, each with a distinct role within the body (1 Peter 1:10).

Despite Christ's elevation of women and societal progress in many cultures, the church has regressed in its treatment of women. During the second century, biases against women resurfaced, leading to their diminished status within the church. The following quotes, attributed to esteemed men of the time, reveal the chauvinistic culture that permeated the church:

- St. Tertullian (about 155 to 225 AD): "Do you not know that you are each an Eve? The sentence of God on this sex of yours lives in this age: the guilt must of necessity live too. You are the Devil's gateway: You are the unsealer of the forbidden tree: You are the first deserter of the divine law: You are she who persuaded him whom the devil was not valiant enough to attack. You destroyed so easily God's image, man. On account of your desert even the Son of God had to die."

- St. Augustine of Hippo (354 to 430 AD). He wrote to a friend: "What is the difference whether it is in a wife or a mother, it is still Eve the temptress that we must beware of in any woman...I fail to see what use woman can be to a man if one excludes the function of bearing children."

- St. Thomas Aquinas (1225 to 1274 AD): "As regards to the individual nature, woman is defective and misbegotten, for the active force in the male seed tends to the production of a perfect likeness in the masculine sex; while the production of woman comes from a defect in the active force or from some material indisposition, or even from some external influence (How can the 'production of woman' come from a defect? She was crafted in the Garden from the hand of the Divine!)."

- Martin Luther (1483 to 1546 AD): "If they [women] become tired or even die, that does not matter. Let them die in childbirth, that's why they are there." Even Luther failed to see the example of Christ who commented that the best thing a woman could do was to follow him, not raise children. I do recognize that Luther may have said this in response to his attack against the Gnostic teaching that believers should refrain from marriage and sex, along with any self-gratification.

These statements serve as a poignant reminder of the challenges women have faced in asserting their rightful place within the church, and the urgent need to dismantle patriarchal structures that hinder the body of Christ from fully embodying its mission and purpose.

A Call for Renewal and Inclusion

The shocking reality of sexism within the church spans over fourteen centuries, from the second century to the sixteenth century and persists to some extent even today. What is truly astonishing is not just the existence of such sentiments but the individuals who voiced them—esteemed figures presumed to have insight into the heart of God. These statements, made by influential men of their time, reveal a glaring blind spot that has perpetuated resentment and exclusion for countless women within society.

Despite claiming to represent God's will, these individuals demonstrated a profound misunderstanding of His teachings, fostering a culture of inequality and disenfranchisement. Their words have left a deep scar on the collective consciousness of women, many of whom long for spiritual intimacy but find themselves alienated by the institutionalized church.

It is understandable that some women reject the church, seeking fulfillment elsewhere as they perceive no place for them within its confines. This void, left by the church's failure to embrace all members of its community, has led to a search for meaning in avenues that do not fully satisfy the soul.

As we confront this history of sexism and exclusion, it is

imperative that we acknowledge the pain it has caused and work towards a more inclusive and equitable future. The church must rediscover its foundational principles of love, acceptance, and equality, ensuring that all individuals, regardless of gender, race, or status, feel valued and empowered within the body of Christ. Only then can we truly embody the teachings of Jesus and fulfill our mission to spread His love and grace to all corners of the world.

"There is neither Jew nor Greek, there is neither slave nor free, there is no male and female, for you are all one in Christ Jesus." Galatians 3:28.

Chapter Eleven Summary

Again, I want to restate that my goal is not to divide. It is to build up, inform, and help set free women who have avoided the institutional church over the years. I want to point them to the Savior, their Creator, who is longing to have a relationship with those he made. And also to say that there are other options for fellowship within the body. In the US, there are many people who have begun gathering in more intimate settings within their homes.

Everyone has been given a gift to use to help build up the body. And everyone has been given a gift to help point the way for the lost. I want to regain my mission, my identity, and to be aware of how much society has impacted the church. I want to stay rooted in the truth so I will not be deceived.

In this chapter, it is evident by the fourth century, things changed within the body of Christ. Christians were no longer persecuted. The church began to look like the pagan culture in their fellowship as it was influenced by the Roman Empire.

Compromise snuck in. So did mediocrity.

Believers lost their mission and became introverted under the institutionalized church. The result was a loss of impact within society. This furthered as the ages went along and Gnosticism and asceticism were taught by early church fathers. The sexes again began to divide. Women were given a place.

Separation in the body was drawn between clergy and laity. The Industrial Revolution was the noose for the family unit in Europe and America. Within a few decades, all were working under capitalism and people began to be consumers. Little was left to be made in the home. What is left today is a generation without identity, huge elevations in mental illness, and an unhealthy manner of living. People go to church to get nurturing, instead of employing their gifts. Churches aren't set up to allow gifts to be used. Pastors are overworked and suffering burnout.

Study questions for chapter eleven:

1. How has the church today been impacted by society?

2. What was once the common denominator for the household, business, and family?

3. What is the implication that almost nothing is made in the household anymore?

4. Why do people suffer more today from mental illness than ever before?

5. Why do a lot of people attend church today?

6. What is the actual definition of the laity?

7. How can one apply what they have learned today?

Key points from chapter eleven:

- The church has impacted culture; culture has impacted the church.
- The early church lived within a social structure without conforming to it.
- Until the past few centuries the household, business, and family had the same identity in most civilizations.
- Work was moved away from the home during the Industrial Revolution.
- People are struggling to find their identity and purpose.
- Fewer people are having children.
- Many people go to church to get emotional support and nurturing.
- Close to 90 percent of American pastors receive counseling from burnout or the feeling of failure.
- This is a sign that organized religion isn't working.
- All followers of Christ are "clergy" or the "inheritance of God."
- Around the second century, the word "laikos" was used to reference "idiotes" or "unprofessionals" in Greek literature.
- Over time it evolved to the word "laity" to reference unprofessional, common, or profane people as opposed to the educated, holy, or sacred select.
- Dualism and sexism undermine the pure nature of the church.

CHAPTER ELEVEN

Closing prayer for chapter eleven:

"Abba, I am so humbled and grieved. I am saddened by how men over the ages have only thought women were good for childbearing. And I don't understand why only Eve is charged with transgressing by such influential men. But I know You said You have made all things new. I know You came to set the captive free. And I know You will make everything beautiful in time. I don't know how to apply this information or the knowledge that the church once again enrolled status and initiated divisions. I long to work alongside my brothers and sisters in faith, to have koinonia. To rejoice when they rejoice, and to weep when they weep. Oh, Abba, please bless me and guide me in these things. Amen."

Chapter Twelve

The Trail Ahead for Women in the Church

*H**ere lands as true a subject, being prisoner, as ever landed at these stairs. Before Thee, O God, I speak it, having none other friend but Thee alone.* —Queen Elizabeth

Jehovah says in Isaiah 40 that all men are like grass. They fade and blow away like dust. No one gives YHWH counsel. No one enlightens him. And it would seem very few long to know the heart of the One who made them. In fact, there is no one easier to get to than Jesus Christ.

Isaiah 40:6-8 highlights the transient nature of humanity compared to the eternal nature of God. It emphasizes that human wisdom and understanding pale in comparison to the wisdom and knowledge of the Creator. Jesus Christ, as the Son of God, offers a direct path for humanity to know and understand the heart of God, providing a way for people to establish a personal relationship with their Creator.

Reflections on the Role of Women in the Early Church and Today

At the onset of the church age, people were of simpler intellect compared to contemporary Western civilization, yet they found their way to the cross with the guidance of the Holy Spirit. However, today's well-educated church often relies more on intellect than spiritual guidance.

Over the centuries, the emphasis on human intellect has led to division within the body of Christ, contrary to the unity fostered by the cross. Despite societal inequalities based on factors like sex, race, and creed, Galatians 3:26-28 affirms the equality of all believers under Christ Jesus, as I quoted at the end of the last chapter.

However, attempting to force women into roles institutionalized by men for men may seem unnatural. The Roman Catholic Church maintains a male-only priesthood based on tradition and interpretation, citing divine law and the perceived masculinity of Jesus and his apostles.

Yet, historical evidence suggests that women served as deacons in the early church, challenging modern interpretations. The Greek word "diakonos" signifies one who serves, suggesting women's involvement in ministry should not be restricted.

Ultimately, the question of women's roles in the church requires careful examination of Scripture, tradition, and the leading of the Holy Spirit to discern God's will for His people, regardless of gender.

Revisiting the Role of Women in Early Church History

During the early church era, evidence suggests that women held significant roles, including that of deaconesses, challenging modern perceptions. The ecumenical First Council of Nicaea in 325 AD acknowledged the existence of deaconesses, although ordination was not deemed necessary for their service. Subsequent councils, such as the Council of Chalcedon in 451 AD, outlined specific criteria for the ordination of deaconesses, further affirming their presence within the church hierarchy.

The word deacon translates to diakonos in Greek. Literally, it is defined as "one who runs through the dust after his master." That's me! Yes!

The roles of deacons and deaconesses differed, with deaconesses primarily serving as caregivers and leading women in sacraments like baptism. While some theologians in the Middle Ages refrained from expressing opinions on female deacons, evidence from early church writings suggests their prominence alongside men in various leadership roles.

Notable biblical figures like Priscilla, Phoebe, and Mary are mentioned as actively serving the Lord, indicating their involvement in ministry. Historical documents, including Pliny's letter to Emperor Trajan and the Didascalia treatise, provide further evidence of the existence and recognition of deaconesses within the early church.

The recognition of women in leadership positions, including deaconesses, highlights a more inclusive approach to ministry in early Christianity. Figures like Macrina, a renowned deaconess who founded her own monastic community, exemplify the significant contributions of women in shaping the early church landscape.

Another deaconess recorded to have begun a monastic community was Melania, born in the latter part of the fourth century. She provided a way station, or shelter, for pilgrims. During this period it became popular for wealthy Christians to make religious pilgrimages to the holy places. These women welcomed virgins and widows, and all single women taking a vow of celibacy. This was highly honorable in those days, as was an austere lifestyle. Sex was thought to be of the flesh; self-control was better. This most certainly was an influence that Gnosticism left on the early church amidst its false teachings.

The Decline of Deaconesses in Church History

As Christianity became institutionalized under Constantine's rule, the position of deaconesses underwent significant changes, diminishing their role and authority within the church. Legalization of Christianity led to a shift towards social prominence, resulting in the submission of women under male-dominated hierarchy, particularly in the Western Empire.

Archaeological and literary evidence from Asia Minor and Constantinople indicates the presence of deaconesses, with notable figures like Olympias serving as influential members of the clergy during the fifth century. The Hagia Sophia, an iconic church building in Istanbul, provides historical context, with deaconesses listed alongside deacons in church documents from the sixth century onward.

In the Byzantine church, deaconesses held both liturgical

and pastoral roles, caring for the imprisoned, persecuted, and attending to various spiritual needs. However, limitations imposed on menstruating women in the seventh century, coupled with ritualistic impurity theology in the eleventh century, led to a decline in the role of deaconesses.

By the twelfth century, the ordination of women had vanished entirely in the Byzantine Church, with further restrictions barring menstruating women from entering churches or receiving the Eucharist. This regression marked a departure from the egalitarian principles of early Christianity, highlighting the institutionalization's adverse effects on women's leadership within the church.

The fourteenth and fifteenth centuries were marked by profound challenges and discord, including the devastating impact of the Black Death and widespread corruption within the church leadership. Amidst these tumultuous times, religious persecutions and uprisings occurred, leading to the suppression of revolutionary thinkers who dared to challenge prevailing orthodoxies.

Today we're censored; I know first hand.

The Turmoil of the Renaissance Church and the Rise of the Protestant Reformation

The Renaissance church of the fourteenth and fifteenth centuries was characterized by spiritual lukewarmness and compromise, marked by corruption and darkness. The era was further marred by the brutality of the Spanish Inquisition, initiated in 1478 by Catholic monarchs Isabella and Ferdinand, who sought to enforce Catholic orthodoxy through military force and coerced conversions.

CHAPTER TWELVE

As dissatisfaction with the religious system grew across Europe, many anticipated an uprising, which eventually materialized in the sixteenth century with the advent of the Protestant Reformation. Martin Luther's Ninety-Five Theses, penned in 1517, marked the beginning of this transformative movement, challenging the Roman Catholic Church's monopoly on religion.

The Reformation sparked fierce debates over various doctrinal issues, including the sale of church positions, purgatory, Mariology, intercession, devotion to saints, the Eucharist, celibacy, and papal authority. Luther's defiance led to his excommunication and forced him into hiding, while his ideas ignited the Peasant's War, resulting in significant casualties among Catholics. Additionally, the Church of England severed ties with Rome during this period.

Despite the tumultuous events of church history, it is evident that God's providence transcends human endeavors. The journey through the annals of the church fathers' decisions, both virtuous and flawed, underscores the penetrating gaze of God into the hearts of humanity. As we reflect on this history, women are empowered with knowledge and enlightenment, enabling them to navigate their positions in contemporary society with gratitude toward their gracious Father and Master.

With the Reformation, the position of women shifted again.

Amidst the tumult of the Reformation, Catholic women found themselves grappling with significant shifts in their roles and identities within the Church. As the Protestant movement gained momentum, some Catholic women emerged as critics, lamenting the perceived loss of their place and influence.

Central to their concerns was the removal of Mary as the primary role model for women, leaving a void in the established norms of behavior. The cessation of the veneration of saints deprived women of female patrons to honor and mediate their spiritual needs. With men assuming dominant roles in church leadership and authority, women felt marginalized and excluded from positions of influence.

Furthermore, the characterization of the pope as the "whore of Babylon" by some reformers was deeply unsettling and challenged the traditional reverence accorded to the papal office. These critiques underscored the destabilizing effects of the Reformation on the established structures of Catholicism and the perceived loss of special places and roles reserved for women within the Church.

Shifting Views on Marriage and Women's Roles During the Reformation

During the Reformation era, profound changes swept through society, particularly regarding marriage and women's roles within it. Embraced as a preferred state over celibacy, marriage was no longer viewed as a weakness but as a natural and honorable institution. Women found liberation from the constant comparison to Eve and were no longer stigmatized for their bodily functions, which were now recognized as part of the natural order.

Martin Luther's teachings promoted marriage equality and emphasized shared household responsibilities. However, his views faced opposition from traditionalists who advocated for female subordination and upheld the classical views of Aristotle.

Martin Bucer emerged as a forward-thinking figure, emphasizing the importance of marriage as the foundation of society and learning. He advocated for mutual respect and self-sacrifice within marriage, challenging rigid notions of divorce and promoting grace and compassion in marital relationships.

John Milton further contributed to the discourse on marriage by advocating for divorce in cases of emotional or intellectual incompatibility, challenging the strict doctrines of the Roman Catholic Church. He emphasized the importance of companionship in marriage and opposed arranged marriages, advocating for freedom and agency in courtship.

Despite these progressive views on marriage, challenges persisted, including domestic violence, adultery, and prostitution, which posed threats to marital stability. Efforts were made to regulate and restrict these practices, reflecting evolving societal attitudes toward marriage and morality during the Reformation era.

Societal Transformations During the Reformation Era

The Reformation era brought about significant shifts in society, impacting family structures, individual consciousness, and economic dynamics.

With the rise of Protestantism, family units in England underwent changes, moving towards two-generational households as grandparents became less involved. The authority of priests diminished, and individual responsibility emerged, altering the traditional dynamics of confession and communion.

The Reformation also influenced attitudes towards witch trials, with periods of resurgence following lulls as attention was focused on religious matters. The trials saw a significant increase in executions, predominantly targeting women. Especially single women and widows with land. It was lucrative to be a church authority.

While marriage remained an economic institution, Martin Luther's proposals for early marriage with parental consent faced resistance, particularly from urban authorities and employers concerned about disruptions to property distribution and labor markets.

Before and during the Reformation, the majority of the population lived in rural areas, where women were engaged in various unskilled labor roles such as agriculture, animal husbandry, and textile manufacturing. The growth of mining further reshaped gender roles, providing new opportunities for men in the workforce.

In the following century, all of the focus was turning to the strange new land across the waters.

Chapter Twelve Summary

This chapter provides valuable insights into the historical shifts in the status of women within the church, from the early Catholic Church to the Protestant Reformation. It highlights how women held significant positions, such as deaconesses, in the early church, only to see their roles restricted in later centuries.

The chapter underscores the transformative impact of the Reformation, which challenged traditional hierarchies and provided newfound liberties for women. It acknowledges the contributions of contemporary advocates of equality and emphasizes the importance of understanding the broader historical context in shaping women's roles within Christianity.

Study questions for chapter twelve:

CHAPTER TWELVE

1. When did the church begin to be institutionalized?

2. What were some of the men saying about the role of women?

3. Was there any proof that women were being ordained or holding the position of deaconesses?

4. What is the word used to mean "one who runs after their master"?

5. When did the role of deaconess really begin to change?

6. When did deaconesses finally disappear from the churches in the East and West?

7. What were some of the advantages of the position that women experienced after the Reformation?

Key points from chapter twelve:

- It is unnatural to force women into a role institutionalized by men.
- A controversy for the ordination of female deaconesses still exists.
- There has been plenty of evidence confirming that women served as deacons in the early church.
- As women were mostly illiterate, deaconesses did not teach men; they functioned as caregivers and led women into water baptism and the like.
- Deaconesses were mentioned in writings during the early church as having the same role as deacons.

- "Diakonein" translates to "minister."
- One can find it describing Mary Magdalene, Joanna, and others in the New Testament.
- An austere lifestyle was encouraged by the church after Constantine.
- Sex was thought to be of the flesh; self-control was better.
- This was an influence of Gnosticism.
- The roles of deaconesses in the Byzantine church were both liturgical and pastoral.
- They also cared for the persecuted church and cared for their emotional and spiritual needs.
- There are frescoes and paintings from the early Christian period depicting women in different ministerial roles.
- The deaconesses' role changed dramatically after the fourth century.
- The church became institutionalized under Constantine.
- The ordination of women vanished by the twelfth century in the Byzantine church.
- Deaconesses disappeared in the eastern Mediterranean churches by the eleventh century and by the twelfth and thirteen centuries they disappeared from the European Christian church.
- The Renaissance church was spiritually lukewarm and full of compromise.
- The Protestant Reformation began under the "Ninety Five Theses" written by Martin Luther in 1517.
- Some of the things disputed in the theses were Mariology, intercession for the saints, the Eucharist, mandatory celibacy, and the authority of the pope.
- Some Catholic women were opposed to the Reformation, saying women lost their place.

- Marriage was considered better than celibacy and no longer a weakness.
- Women were being freed from being compared to "wretched Eve" as men were recognized to sin as much as women.
- Luther encouraged equality in marriage and the sharing of household duties.
- John Milton, author of "Paradise Lost", wrote pamphlets encouraging that divorce be permitted in an incompatible marriage. He himself divorced for this reason.
- Unions outside of marriage were discouraged and discriminated against within society and the church.

Closing prayer for chapter twelve:

"Abba, You alone are Faithful and True. You are the Giver of good gifts. And You do all things well. Thank You that you allow women to "run after their master." Thank You that you have guided and protected us over the ages. Thank You, too, for the Reformation and all that it meant to women. Thank You that I'm under Christ; I wouldn't want to be under any other authority, all are equal. Thank You that he is my source, my living water. Please guide me into all truth according to the power that works within me. Amen."

Conclusion

I hope that I've given you some food for thought and that you've had a little snack! It's truly heartening to reflect on the profound impact that "What Every Woman Should Know" has had on my life and faith journey. My path through the pages of this book has been enlightening, challenging, and deeply enriching.

As I've delved into its contents, I've come to appreciate the depth and complexity of theology, and I've gained a deeper understanding of the cultural context and historical background of the Bible. This deeper understanding has opened my eyes to the brilliance of Christ's teachings and his revolutionary impact on society, particularly in his relationships with women.

One of the most valuable lessons I've learned is not to read my own culture into the word of God but to seek purity and understanding in his message. Understanding the context of the Bible and its cultural nuances has been incredibly fruitful for me, allowing me to see familiar passages in new and enlightening ways.

I've also been encouraged to explore scripture further through a chronological reading of the Bible and to consider experiencing the Holy Land firsthand. These experiences have the potential to bring the Bible to life in a whole new way and deepen my connection to its teachings.

As I continue on my journey of faith and growth, I'm grateful for the peace and insight that this book has brought me. My hope is that others may also benefit from its wisdom and discover something invaluable that every woman should know.

Afterword

This book is a compilation of an older work put in a new light. Coming soon is the second volume in the What Every Woman Should Know series. While Volume I shed light on equality in the Scripture leaving us with a quick overview of equality in church history, Volumen II carries on where Volume I left off. In it, we will get a rich taste of women's place as the centuries unfolded.

Yes, indeed. The challenges we face today, such as the curse of the fatherless generation, are deeply intertwined with the historical and cultural contexts we've explored. The breakdown of the family unit, the shifting roles and expectations within society, and the erosion of traditional values all contribute to this modern dilemma.

The absence of fathers, whether due to physical absence, emotional distance, or other factors, leaves a significant void in the lives of many individuals. This absence can have profound effects on children, leading to issues such as insecurity, emotional instability, and a lack of positive male role models.

As we navigate these complex issues, it's essential to draw upon the timeless wisdom found in scripture and to seek guidance from the teachings of Christ. By fostering strong, nurturing families and communities, and by providing support and mentorship to those in need, we can work towards healing the wounds of the fatherless generation and building a brighter future for all.

What does the future look like for women? Will we know equality on this side of heaven? What's the fourfold purpose of marriage?

I'll hope you have an appetite for What Every Woman Should Know: Volumen II: The Way Forward when it's available. And have some more food for thought!

AFTERWORD

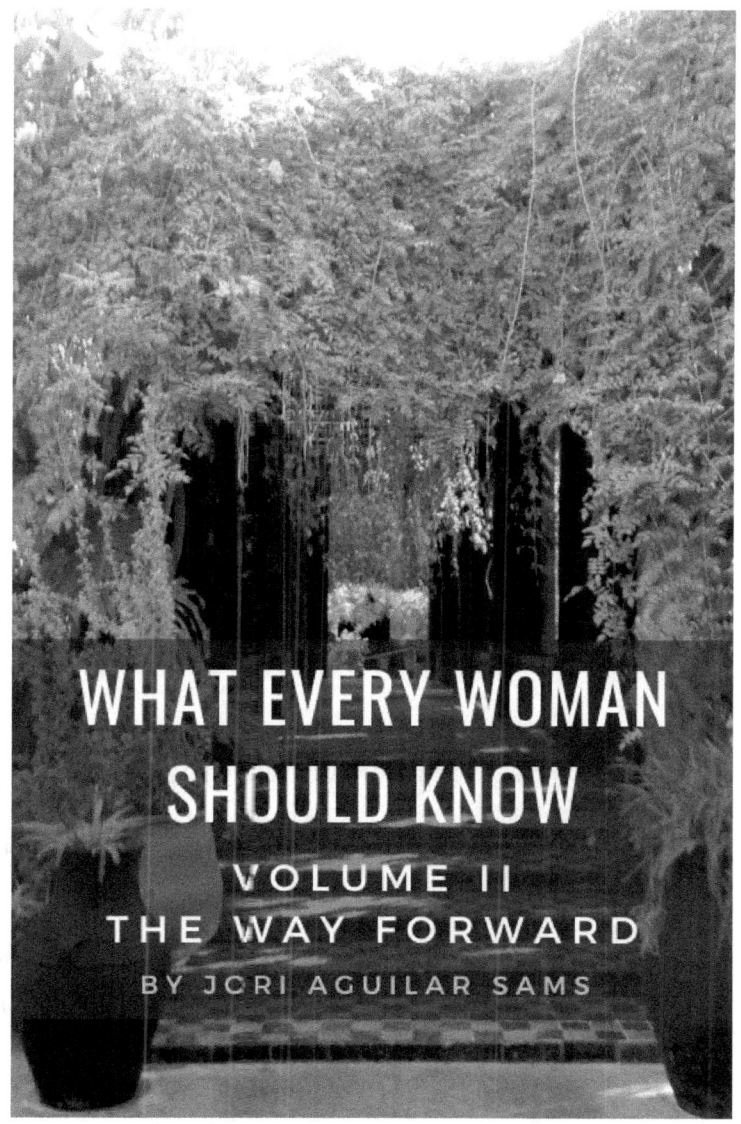

Bibliography for What Every Woman Should Know Volumes I and II

"Abortion Facts." The Center for Bio-Ethical Reform. February 2010. <http://www.abortionno.org/Resources/fastfacts.html>.

"Academic: Gender Equality." India. February 2010. <http://www.uoguelph.ca/cids/indiasemestr/equality.html>.

Alexander, David L. "A Rose by Any Other Name." Eternal Word Television Network.
    January 2009. <http://www.ewtn.org/library/LITURGY/AROSEBY.TXT>.

Allen, Christopher. "Traditions Weigh on China's Women." BBC News. 19 June 2006. April 2009. <http://news.bbc.co.uk/2/hi/5086754.stm>.

Anderson, Nancy. C. "The Changing Roles of Women in Asia." Asia
    Sentinel. 23 October 2006. May 2009. <http://www.asiasen

tinel.com/index.php?
  option=com_content&task=view&id=232&Itemid=258>.

Barak, Gregg, Paul Leighton, and Jeanne Flavin. "Class, Race, Gender, and Crime: The Social Realities of Justice in America." Google Books/Roman and Littlefield. January 2010. <http://books.google.es/books?id=a-OT3cOQuGAC>.

Barnard, Amy. "Adultery Statistics." Shrinkwrap Resource. 23 December, 2007. February 2010. <http://hfbcshrinkwrap.wordpress.com/2007/12/23/adultery-statisitics/>.

Barrick, Audrey. "Teen Trend Predictions for 2008." Christian Post. 3 January 2008. January 2010. <http://www.christianpost.com/news/teen-trend- predictions-for-2008-
  30721/>.

Bellis, Mary. "History of the Brassiere." About. February 2010.
  <http://inventors.about.com/od/bstartinventions/a/brassiere.htm>.

— — — — — — - " Who Invented Pantyhose?" About. February 2010.
  <http://inventors.about.com/od/qstartinventions/a/pantyhose.htm>.

Bezlova, Antoanета. "China to Formalize One-Child Policy." Asia Times Online. 24 May 2001. 26 October 2011 . <http://www.atimes.com/china/CE24Ad02.html>.

Bose, Mandakranta. "Faces of the Feminine in Ancient, Me-

195

dieval and
Modern India." Google Books/Oxford University Press. February 2010. < http://books.google.es/books?id=lNOUSo6Eb-oC>.

Burns, Alan J. "The Potter and His Clay." Google Books/Xulon Press.
February 2010. <http://books.google.es/books?id=YloZdbUOZ9cC>.

Calvin, John. "Calvin's Commentaries: Complete." WikiSource. April 2009.
<http://en.wikisource.org/wiki/Calvin%E2%80%99s_CommentariesE2%80%94Complete/Genesis_1-23/Chapter_19>.

Chambers, Oswald. 2000. "The Complete Works of Oswald Chambers." Grand Rapids: Discovery House Publishers.

"Cheating Husband: Facts and Advice." Truth About Deception. February 2010. <http://www.truthaboutdeception.com/cheating-and-
infidelity/stats-about-infidelity/cheating-husband.html>.

"Chinese Cultural Studies." Brooklyn College Core Web Pages. February 2010.
<http://acc6.its.brooklyn.cuny.edu/~phalsall/texts/chinwomn.html>.

Choate, J.C. "The Law of God." What Do the Scriptures Say.
June 2009. <http://www.scripturessay.com/article.php?cat=&id=637>.

Clark, Elizabeth Ann. "Women in the Early Church." Google Books/Liturgical Press

Cline, Austin. "Saudi Women and Hypocrisy." About. 17 March 2006. February 2010.
<http://atheism.about.com/b/2006/03/17/saudi-women-and-hypocrisy.htm>.

"Commentary Critical and Explanatory on the Whole Bible." Christian
Classics Ethereal Library. May 2009. <http://www.ccel.org/ccel/jamieson/jfb.x.v.xxii.html#x.v.xxii- p0.1>.

"Compare the Caste System..." Wikispaces. May 2009.
<https://apworld.wikispaces.com/Compare+the+caste+system+to+other+systemssical+civilizations>.

"Courtly Love." Wikipedia. February 2010. <http://en.wikipedia.org/wiki/Courtly_love>.

"Did Jephthah sacrifice his daughter to the Lord?" Got Questions?. 1 July 2009. <http://www.gotquestions.org/Jephthahs-daughter.html>.

"Divorce and Remarriage." Religious Tolerance.
February 2010. <http://www.religioustolerance.org/chr_dira.htm>.

"Doctors Call for Weight Loss Industry Regulation." CBC News. 17 February 2009. February 2010.

197

<http://www.cbc.ca/news/canada/calgary/story/2009/02/17/weight-
loss.html?ref=rss>.

Dave Miller Ph.D. "Jephthah's Daughter." Apologetic Press. 1 July 2009. <http://www.apologeticspress.org/articles/2320>.

Dr. Lotter. "Menopause: The Last Blood Rite." Tides of Life. April 2009. <http://www.tidesoflife.com/bloodrite.htm>.

Ehtisham, S MD. "Status of Muslim Women: A Historic Review." Counter
Currents. 24 March, 2007. May 2009. <http://www.counter currents.org/gen- ehtisham240307.htm>.

El Saadawi, Nawa. 1980. "The Hidden Face of Eve." Boston: Beacon
Press.

Elwell, Walter A. 1996. "Baker's Evangelical Dictionary of Biblical
Theology: Family Life and Relations." Grand Rapids: Baker Books.

"Fashion Industry Stats." GrabStats.
February 2010. <http://www.grabstats.com/statcategorymain.asp? StatCatID=12>.

"Fighting Isms and Schisms." Christian History and Biography. 1 July 1987. January 2010.
<http://www.ctlibrary.com/ch/1987/issue15/1529.html>.

"Giving Statistics." Church Tithes and Offerings. 11 December 2008. January 2010.
  <http://churchtithesandofferings.com/blog/giving-statistics/>.

"Glossary of Philosophical Isms." VisWiki. January 2010.
  <http://www.viswiki.com/en/Glossary_of_philosophical_isms>.

Goldstein, Elyse. 2008. "The Women's Torah Commentary." Jewish Lights
  Publication.

Grant, L M. "Wisdom's Closing Message." Biblecentre. February 2010.
  <http://www.biblecentre.org/commentaries/lmg_24_prov_ch_31.htm>.

Guin, Jay. "Buried Talents: Women in the Old Testament, Part I." One in
  Jesus. 8 April 2008. April 2009. <http://oneinjesus.info/2008/04/18&nbs
  /buried-talents-women-in-the-old-testament-part-1-the-law-and-miriam/>.

Henry, Matthew. "Matthew Henry's Commentary." Christian Notes. April 2009. <http://www.christnotes.org/commentary.php?
  com=mhc&b=46&c=11>.

Hicks, John Mark. "Women in the Assembly." John Mark Hicks

Ministries. 20 February 2009. March 2009.
<http://johnmarkhicks.wordpress.com/2009/02/20/women-in-the-assembly-
1-corinthians-1434-35/>.

"HIV Women Forced Into Sex for Treatment in India." AsiaOne. 22 December 2007. February 2010.
<http://www.asiaone.com/Just%2BWoman/News/Women%2BIn%2BThe%2BNews/Story/l>.

Hocker, George E. Jr. "Break the Agony and Bondage of Pornographic Addiction." Love Takes Time. February 2010. <http://www.lovetakestime.com/art- breaktheagony.html>.

"Infidelity Statistics." Infidelity Facts. 2006. February 2010. <http://www.infidelityfacts.com/infidelity- statistics.html>.

"Infidelity Statistics." Menstuff. February 2010.
<http://www.menstuff.org/issues/byissue/infidelitystats.html>.

"Israeli Life." Visions of Israel. 2008. February 2010. <http://visionsof.org/israel/culture/israellife.html>.

Jackson, Wayne. "To What Law Were the Ancient Gentiles Accountable?"
Christian Courier. June 2009. <http://www.christiancourier.com/articles/759-to-what-law- were-the-ancient-gentiles-accountable>.

Jagers, J. Lee, PhD, ThM, LPC. "God's Purpose for Marriage: A

Biblical

View." J. Lee Jagers, PhD, ThM, LPC. February 2010. <http://leejagers.wordpress.com/2008/04/01/gods- purpose-for-marriage-a-biblicalview/>.

"Jesus-Themed Cosmetics Draw the Wrath of the Righteous." Hairfinder. 16 February 2008. February 2010.
<http://www.hairfinder.com/news/20080302.htm>.

JPH. "Did Jephthah Really Sacrifice His Daughter?" Tekton. 1 July 2009. <http://www.tektonics.org/gk/jepthah.html>.

Katz, Neil Samson; Sherry, Marisa. "India: The Missing Girls." PBS.
26 April 2007. February 2010.
<http://www.pbs.org/frontlineworld/rough/2007/04/the_missing_gir.html>.

Kay, Glenn. "Jewish Wedding Custom and Bride of Messiah." Messianic
Fellowship. April 2009. <http://messianicfellowship.50webs.com/wedding.html>.

Keathley, J. Hampton III. "The Mosaic Law: It's Function and Purpose in the
New Testament." Bible. June 2009. <http://bible.org/article/mosaic-law-its-function-and- purpose-new-testament>.

King, Philip J., and Lawrence E. Stager. "Life in Biblical Israel." Google
Books/Westminster John Knox Press. June 2009. <http://bo

oks.google.es/books?id=OtOhypZz_pEC>.

Kroeger, Catherine Clark. "The IVP Women's Bible Commentary." Google
   Books/InterVaristy Press. February 2010. <http://books.google.es/books?id=dCdeeYC3obkC>.

Kruse, Michael W. "Household of God." Kruse Kronicle.
   8 May 2007. April 2009. <http://krusekronicle.typepad.com/kruse_kronicle/2007/05/index_to_househ.html>.

Kukkee, Raymond Alexander. "On the Failure of Relationships." Associated Content.
   14 October 2008. February 2010.
   <http://plato.stanford.edu/entries/time/>.

Lee-Potter, Linda. "The Price We Will Pay for a Fatherless Generations." Mail Online.
   February 2010. < http://www.dailymail.co.uk/news/article-59485/The- price-pay-fatherless-generation.html>.

Legath, Jennifer Anne Wiley. 2008. "The Phoebe Phenomenon." Ann
   Arbor:UMI.

Lester, Meera. "The Everything Mary Magdalene Book..." Google
   Books/Everything Books.

June 2009. <http://books.google.es/books?id=c2Blkd6uTaoC>.
Lewis, Angie. "8 Biblical Facts About Marriage." Ezine.

February 2010. <http://ezinearticles.com/?8-Biblical-Facts-About-Marriage&id=78750>.

Lile, William Dr. "Dr. Lile Partial Birth Abortion Demo." YouTube. 20 April 2006. February 2010. <http://www.youtube.com/watch?v=s_W75zh1j2I>.

Linder, Douglas. "A History of Witchcraft Persecutions." Law2 UMKC. 1 August 2009.<http://law2.umkc.edu/faculty/projects/ftrials/salem/witchhistory.html>.

Lindley, Susan Hill. "You Have Stepped Out of Your Place." Google
   Books/Westminster John Knox Press. May 2009. <http://books.google.es/books?id=gBIPJiXRcZUC>.

Linsley, Alice C. "C.S. Lewis on Women Priests." Students Publish Here.
   22 January 2009. March 2009.
   <http://teachgoodwriting.blogspot.com/2009/01/cs-lewis-on-women-
   priests.html>.

Lussier, Ernest S.S.S. "Daily Life in Ancient Israel." Catholic Culture. June 2009. <http://www.catholicculture.org/culture/library/view.cfm?
   Id=1356&CFID=18239044&CFTOKEN=67477905>.

"Married Women's Property Act 1870." Wikipedia. May 2009.
   <http://en.wikipedia.org/wiki/Married_Women%27s_Property_Act_1870>.

"Matters of Scale: Spending Priorities." Worldwatch Institute. February 2010. <http://www.worldwatch.org/node/764>.

"Matthew 5 - IVP New Testament Commentaries." BibleGateway. February 2010.
   <http://www.biblegateway.com/resources/commentaries/IVP-NT/Matt/Do-
   Not-Betray-Your-Spouse>.

Metcalf, Barbara Daly and Thomas R. "A Concise History of Modern
   India." Google Books/Cambridge University Press.
   February 2010. <http://books.google.es/books?id=iuESgYNYPl0C>.

Micky1230. "Biological Differences Between Women and Men." Socyberty. 25 February 2009. 23 June 2009.
   <http://www.socyberty.com/Sociology/Biological-Differences-Between-
   Women-and-Men.555409>.

Moll, Rob. "Scrooge Lives." Christianity Today.
   5 December 2008. January 2010.
   <http://www.christianitytoday.com/ct/2008/december/10.24.html?start=3>.

Momlogic I. "Is Bisexuality a Teen Trend?" Gather. 12 June 2008. January 2010.
   <http://www.gather.com/ articleId=281474977371307>.

"Nearly 40% of Nepali Women Trafficked..." Modern Tribalist. 2 August 2007. February 2010. <http://moderntribalist.blogs

pot.com/2007/08/nearly-40-of-nepali-women-trafficked.html>.

Newsom, Carol Ann, and Sharon H. Ringe. "Women's Bible Commentary." Google Books/Westminster John Knox Press. April 2009. <http://books.google.es/books?id=vF89aBJTo0cC>.

Okin, Susan Moller. "Justice, Gender and the Family." Google Books.
January 2010. <http://books.google.es/books?id=wl3R1rYDqP8C>.

Olsen, Kirstin. "A Chronology of Women's History." Google Books/Greenwood Publishing Group. January 2010. <http://books.google.es/books?id=jFY3CxmHk4cC>.

"Ordination of Women." Wikipedia. January 2010. <http://en.wikipedia.org/wiki/Ordination_of_women>.

"PMC Statement on World Population Day." Population Media Center. 10 July 2009. February 2010. <http://www.populationmedia.org/2009/07/10/pmc-celebrates-world-population-day/>.

Polhemus, Robert M. 1980 "Cosmic Faith: Lot's daughters: sex, redemption, and women's quest for authority." Chicago: University of Chicago Press.
"Possible Physical Side Effects." American Pregnancy Association. February 2010.
<http://www.americanpregnancy.org/unplannedpregnancy/possiblesideeffects.html>.

205

Preato, Dennis J. "Women Keep Silent." God's Word to Women. March 2009. <http://www.godswordtowomen.org/Preato2.htm>.

"Prenatal Image Gallery." The Endowment for Human Development. February 2010. <http://www.ehd.org/prenatal-images-index.php>

"Realism vs. Idealism in Relationships." The Dating Dope. 7 September 2009. February 2010. <http://www.thedatingdope.com/realism-vs-idealism-in-relationships/>.

Reardon, David C. "After Effects of Abortion." Elliot Institute. 1990. February 2010.
   <http://www.abortionfacts.com/reardon/after_effects_of_abortion.asp>.

Reid, Amy. "Janet Boynes: Lesbian Lifestyle Left Behind." 700 Club. January 2009. January 2010.<http://www.cbn.com/700club/features/amazing/janet_boynes020509.aspx>.

"Relativism and Agnosticism Have Led to Crisis in Marriage and the Family, Cardinal Says." Catholic News Agency. 19 February 2007. February 2010.
   <http://m.catholicnewsagency.com/new.php?n=8673>.

Richardson, Deidra. "Women Deacons In The East, Part V: Later Texts Bearing On Earlier Evidence." Men and Women in the Church. 20 October 2009. January 2010. <http://womeninthechurch-junia.blogspot.com/2009/10/women-deacons-in-east-partv-later.html>.

Robinson, B.A. "The Status of Women on the Gospels." Religious Tolerance.
  March 2009. <http://www.religioustolerance.org/cfe_bibl.htm>.

"Romance." Wikipedia. February 2010. <http://en.wikipedia.org/wiki/Romance_%28love%29>.

"SA Battle Over Muslim Women's Rights." BBC News. 10 September 2009. January 2010.
  <http://news.bbc.co.uk/2/hi/africa/8237097.stm>.

Schwartz, Howard. "Hair and Beauty Salons are Booming Nationwide." Agora Business Center. 2005. February 2010. <http://www.agora-business- center.com/0805salons.htm>.

Sheen, Fulton J. MSGR. 1947. "Communism and Women." CatholicApologetics. February 2010. <http://www.catholicapologetics.info/morality/general/cwoman.htm>.

Sider, Ronald J. "The Scandal of Evangelical Conscience." Books and Culture.
  February 2010. <http://www.booksandculture.com/articles/2005/janfeb/3.8.html>.

Sorokin, Pitirim Aleksandrovich. "Social and Cultural Dynamics." Google
  Books/Transaction Books. January 2010. <http://books.google.es/books?id=fbZyka2W1cC>.

"Statistics and Information on Pornography in the US." Blazing

Grace. February 2010. <http://www.blazinggrace.org/cms/bg/pornstats>.

"The First Civilizations." Neolithic Revolution. May 2009. <http://www.historiasiglo20.org/egypt/proyector%5Btimeline%5D.htm>.

"The History of High Heels." Heikes Heels. February 2010. <http://www.heikes-heels.de/english/history- shoes/1.htm>.

"The History of the Bikini." TimePhotos. February 2010. <http://www.time.com/time/photogallery/0,29307,1908353,00.html>.

"The Marriage, Divorce, Remarriage Cycle." Socyberty. February 2010. <http://socyberty.com/relationships/the-marriage-divorce-remarriage-cycle/>.

"The Protestant Reformation of Women." Free Republic. January 2010. <http://www.freerepublic.com/focus/f-religion/1117035/posts>.

"The Salem Witch Trials of 1692." Law2 UMKC. August 2009. <http://law2.umkc.edu/faculty/projects/ftrials/salem/SALEM.HTM>.
Thompson, James C., B.A., M.Ed.

"Time." Stanford Encyclopedia of Philosophy. 26 February 2008. January 2010. <http://plato.stanford.edu/entries/time/>.

Turner, Brian S. "The Body and Society: Explorations in Social Theory." Google Books.
   May 2009. <http://books.google.es/books?id=K_8WxOqOWtMC>.

Vaswani, Karishma. "India Sees Rise of Independent Women." BBC News. April 2006. February 2010. <
   http://news.bbc.co.uk/2/hi/business/4808200.stm>.

Weinrich, William. "Women in Church History." Historical Renewal. 2006. January 2010.
   <http://www.historicalrenewal.com/articles/women_church_history_P1.htm>.

West, Jim ThD. "Ancient Israelite Marriage Customs." Quartz Hill School of
   Theology. April 2009. <http://www.bible-history.com/links.php cat=2&sub=397&cat_name=Ancient+Israel&sub-cat_name=Manners+%26+Customs>.

"What Females Want." PBS. 24 June 2009. <http://www.pbs.org/wnet/nature/episodes/what-females- want/real-swingers-oftheanimal-kingdom/831/>.

Wicks, Robert J., and Richard D Parsons. "Clinical Handbook of Pastoral
   Counselling." Google Books/Paulist Press. June 2009. <http://books.google.es/books?id=YDFTl16J-sQC>.

Wickstrom, Steven. "Praying Together as a Couple." Columns Crossmap. February 2010. <http://columns.crossmap.com/article/praying-together- as-a- couple/steven-

209

wickstrom/60.htm>.

Winkel, Rich. "Status of Women in Israel." Hartford HWP. 19 February 1997. February 2010. <http://www.hartford-hwp.com/archives/51b/019.html>.

"Women as Property." Bulletproof Pimp. 2 March 2008. May 2009. http://bulletproofpimp.blogspot.com/2008/03/women-as-property.html>.

"Women in Ancient Egypt." Crystal Links. May 2009. <http://www.crystalinks.com/egyptianwomen.html>.

"Women in Patriarchal Societies." International World History Project. May 2009. <http://history-world.org/Civilization,%20women_in_patriarchal_societies.htm>.

"Women in the Bible." Bible Anomalies. March 2009. <http://www.bibleufo.com/anomwomen.htm>.

"World History – Ancient History." Infoplease. 24 June 2009. <http://www.infoplease.com/ipa/A0001196.html>.

"Worst Countries for Women Identified." Under the Hill. 29 October 2009. February 2010. <http://underthehill.wordpress.com/2009/10/29/worst-countries-for-women-identified-all-muslim-global-gender-gap-index-revealed/>.

Thank You!

I hope you have enjoyed your Writeious Book! And that you've had a little snack! Thanks for your support. I hope I can serve you some food for thought again! Visit us at the Writeious Books webpage...https://writeiousbook.com/sp or drop us a line at admin@writeious.com.

About the Author

My mind is always in writer's mode. I feel most grounded when I'm doing just that. This is when I have a chance to give back all that's been invested in me. Spiced with a past that has led me to live in states all over the US, as well as four different countries across Europe, this has supplied me a palette full of colors providing plenty of material to sing and write about. "But by the Grace of God go I!" Create. Inspire. Repeat!

You can connect with me on:
- https://writeious.com/sp
- https://twitter.com/WriteiousBooks
- https://www.facebook.com/Writeious-Books

Also by Jori Aguilar Sams

Jori Sams writes a fine selection of books ranging from fun and light travel fiction to poetry and real heady stuff that will provoke, inspire, and lift your soul.

What Every Woman Should Know: Volume II - The Way Forward
What was God thinking when he made man and woman? Take a journey with me back in time to explore the heart of God, who wants to be intimately acquainted with those he made. This is a new edition in the two-volume series. What you

Unpack some of the most controversial passages in the Bible before embarking on a journey through history to see the changing role of women over the ages. The discoveries may astound you and they just might set you free.

The Great Lockdown Journals: Losing the Old Normal as the World was Bound

With my heart in my mouth, I put the pandemic under the lens. One single virus stopped the world from spinning, causing a global economic shutdown. We have been scared, scourged, and separated. The Great Lockdown is a telling book examining the contagion along with its mysterious onset and the rising controversies connected to it that are deeply dividing as the insurmountable mess gets bigger. What happens next?

The Hustle

Chris and Hue Childs find themselves caught up in a frenzied race to keep up with a succession of dubious guides and chauffeurs leading them on a frantic trail from the Rif Mountains and Chefchaouen to Fes, the Sahara, Todra Gorge, and Marrakech. Braving dilapidated buses, overcrowded taxis, and runaway camels, Hueâ€™s journey has much of the quest about it. A quest to overcome the haggling, the fear of abduction, the certainty that she is being duped, scammed, and hustled at every turn, in search for the authentic Moroccan experience which continually gives her the slip.

Revelation in Seven Weeks: Teacher's Guide: A Bible Study

Is the world heading for global disaster? Are pandemics and contagions a sign that we're approaching the end times?

Do you hold on to fear instead of hope? An in-depth study of the most compelling book in the Bible, Revelation, will move the reader forward in their understanding of these things. And maybe just take the fear out of life.

These daily devotions are easy to digest, intense, and sometimes riveting. This leader's guide is designed to lead the group or those studying alone to discover the rich prophecy of Revelation. It is a must-read for those interested in the prophetic, wanting to predict future events. Get informed today. Don't be taken by surprise!

www.ingramcontent.com/pod-product-compliance
Lightning Source LLC
LaVergne TN
LVHW051550070426
835507LV00021B/2502